JOURNALISM AS A DEMOCRATIC ART

SELECTED ESSAYS BY
COLE C. CAMPBELL

EDITED BY TONY WHARTON

Kettering Foundation Press

Cole Charles Campbell *(Aug. 10, 1953 — Jan. 5, 2007) was a leading voice in American journalism for more than 20 years.*

At the time of his death, he was dean and professor at the Donald W. Reynolds School of Journalism and Center for Advanced Media Studies, University of Nevada, Reno, Nevada. He served as a director of the Kettering Foundation, Dayton, Ohio, and as a fellow at the Poynter Institute for Media Studies, St. Petersburg, Florida. During his newspaper career, he was editor-in-chief, St. Louis Post Dispatch, *St. Louis, Missouri; editor, the* Virginian-Pilot, *Norfolk, Virginia; associate managing editor, Greensboro* News & Record, *Greensboro, North Carolina; assistant city editor, the* News & Observer, *Raleigh, North Carolina; editor, the* Daily Tar Heel, *University of North Carolina, Chapel Hill, North Carolina; and Pulitzer Prize juror, 1993, 1994, 1997, and 1998.*

He is survived by his widow, Catherine L. Werner and their son Clarke; a daughter, Claire, by a previous marriage; and his sisters Constance C. Brough and Catherine J. Campbell.

CONTENTS

IF NOT NOW, WHEN?

Foreword:
Fighting the Good Fight

By Richard C. Harwood

THE MOMENT I THINK OF COLE CAMPBELL, a smile comes over me. He was a delightful person—a savvy conversationalist, instantaneously ready with an insightful quip, a sharer of anything he had. And he had so much to share.

But then, quickly, something deeper comes over me. For what I loved about Cole, and why I came to so deeply admire and respect him over the years, is that he was always in *dogged pursuit* of something meaningful, something vital, about our individual and collective lives.

We live in a time when so many of us are trying to run harder and faster just to keep up; when we feel unrelenting pressure to focus on our daily to-do lists; when our own urge within ourselves to step forward in life can be discarded, denied, or denigrated by others.

And yet, there was Cole Campbell, in dogged pursuit of some larger mission in life.

In this collection of his writings, you will come across some of those pursuits—his thoughts about the contours and public purpose of knowledge, the role of journalism and the journalist in society, and conceptions of public life and community, among others.

As a society, we need these writings—perhaps even more now than when Cole originally wrote each of them. For our politics has reached new levels of toxicity. Public discourse writ large is driven by acrimony and divisiveness. There are few institutions or organizations or leaders Americans trust nowadays. In many respects, many of our communities lack the very capacities—the leaders, organizations, networks, and norms—necessary to create the kind of community that reflects people's shared aspirations and focuses on their chief concerns.

And many communities lack the healthy information environments people need to engage, become informed, and work together.

Journalism and journalists are pivotal in this changing environment. In people's daily lives, they are struggling to see and hear one another, especially those different from themselves. Amid the deafening noise of public life, there is the hope to make sense of the issues and shifting conditions around them. And people long for a sense of possibility; they are tired and wary of all the negativity and gridlock, and they want to hear different perspectives on ways to move ahead.

These are basic human yearnings. They involve how people see themselves and their relationship to others and the ability to form effective and resilient communities together. These yearnings are about how people bring themselves to the public square and engage and connect with others.

Basic human yearnings: these are the matters of Cole's work and life.

But his work was not always easily understood or embraced by others. Still vivid are my own memories of watching individuals and crowds of people listen to Cole speak about such pursuits. Some thought that he was operating outside the nitty-gritty of reality, others that his head was up in the clouds. While a fair share of his fellow journalists applauded his efforts, many more scratched their heads and wondered aloud about what all the talk and debate was about. It wasn't always easy to bring Cole's ideas down to ground level, or to readily make the implications clear, or to translate them into immediate, practical use.

———

Cole knew all this. And yet he kept going.

Over the years his own momentum and trajectory and influence would grow and deepen—notwithstanding some of the hard personal and professional falls he had along the way, many in plain sight for others to see.

But each time he got back up.

His pursuits—those matters of the heart and mind that drove him at his core—weren't about empty ruminations, or idle notions, or lofty ideals. Nor did they spring from some youthful naiveté about life, or fanciful vision of a society untethered from reality.

Cole insisted that his work be practical and relevant.

Simply put, Cole's work was about people, their lives, and the relationship of his profession to them. He did not see himself as a passive bystander in these pursuits. He never envisioned himself as a detached observer. He always had skin in the game.

For Cole, this was a *fight*.

It was a fight about the kind of society people want to create together. In his mind, as in my own, this was a process that could happen only when people came together to identify their common concerns; to argue and debate and deliberate on the choices they face, and the differences among us, even the deep-seated conflicts. It was about people in communities determining for themselves how they wished to move ahead. For Cole, democracy was not for the faint of heart, or for mere cheerleaders, but for active and engaged citizens.

It was also a fight within journalism about the heart of journalism. What was the purpose and role of journalism? How could journalists examine their own conventions and habits and the ways in which they could best contribute to society, knowing full well that old habits die hard?

When it comes to journalism and its relationship to public life, Cole was brave enough to be among a small cadre of catalysts to bring about a larger conversation in the nation about these matters. Then, amid much pushback, he was there to help keep the conversation going, to maintain a level of engagement with others, and always—*always*—to bring his full self to the table. This was not always easy for Cole, because as a thinker and change-agent himself, he had to withstand barbs and criticisms and distortions about his own motives.

But Cole never ran from the work at hand.

If you were to follow him around in his various daily jobs and listen in as he wrestled with ideas and practical applications, you would experience a man who strived to operate with a special kind of intentionality. This is an important topic in my own work. I am partial to a definition of intentionality that is made up of two pieces:

First, that we are wakeful in what we do, attentive, "in the game," present—that we are visible to ourselves and others;

Second, that we see and embrace a moral responsibility for what we say and do—that we understand that our actions matter and there are consequences, which ripple out in all directions from them.

Cole operated intentionally because he believed change in society—namely, in journalism and public life—was so necessary. Anyone who came into contact with Cole knew immediately that he held little interest in working at the margins, or in fiddling around, or, worse yet, in *pretending* to be doing something of value.

I know this because over a span of 20 years or so, beyond the many conversations we had together, I also found myself working with him in the trenches of newsrooms and news operations. For instance, when my colleagues and I worked with Cole at the *Virginian-Pilot*, one of the early efforts in the news industry to deepen a newspaper's relevance and significance in the life of a community, Cole didn't simply deputize someone to do the work and then leave the scene. He was there each and every day—his hair often an utter mess, his wrinkled shirt seemingly just pulled from a pile of clothes, his infamous stack of books and papers towed along as helpful references.

Day after day Cole came ready to engage, sitting up at the table, with his big body sprawled out, and his endless energy providing a sense that we were all on an important mission together. He would openly argue with his colleagues and me about what it means for journalists to really know their community; indeed, he was fearless in ripping apart and putting back together journalistic conventions about who in a community needs to be engaged and in what ways. To Cole, everything was on the table, even if it meant a whole lot more work for him, and even if it meant making himself vulnerable to others.

Cole sought to understand and define what it would truly mean for journalism to be authentic in covering (and engaging) people and their communities. He kept testing whether people in the community—readers and potential readers alike—could see and hear themselves in the journalist's work. He wanted people to know the newspaper held affection for the community, even when holding up a mirror to the community about difficult, even taboo issues. He sought to know whether people felt their experiences were reflected in what was being produced.

None of Cole's efforts were about kowtowing to the community or advertisers or city fathers, or figuring out what news to cover by conducting some marketing study, or playing up to a foundation just because they might plop a grant in his lap. No, Cole took an alternate path—a path that asked people in communities to take ownership of their communities.

Cole believed in community.

He also felt strongly that journalists must take ownership of their part of the relationship in the community. Over time, Cole came to place more and more emphasis on the intrinsic promises and pledges journalists themselves make to communities in their work. Here, again, he was leading us to think about the essence of a journalistic enterprise and its relationship to the larger society.

Over the years I had the good fortune to watch Cole grow and deepen his thinking and his approaches. After the *Virginian-Pilot*, my colleagues and I worked with him when he was editor of the *St. Louis Post-Dispatch*. Cole also was involved in the Journalism Values Institute and other initiatives of the American Society of Newspaper Editors that I helped to lead. My relationship with Cole continued throughout his time with the Kettering Foundation, his various job searches, and then at Reno.

What I came to know about Cole was that above all else he was committed to the pursuit of journalism enterprises that transcended organizational goals of profit and power and position. He knew these things had their rightful place; but Cole's first order of business was to work on the relationship of journalism to a democratic society.

He believed in people and their innate ability to move communities forward.

Perhaps it's too easy or trite to say that Cole wanted to make a difference in the world. But when all is said and done, that's where I end up. It wasn't that he wanted to be "somebody," but to enable others to become themselves. It wasn't that he wanted his own journalistic enterprises to be the center of attention; rather he wanted to experiment and innovate with others so society itself would work better. It wasn't that he sought out awards; instead, he was rewarded by seeing others grow and expand their own reach.

Like all of us, Cole was not without his own ego, his own set of blinders, and his own foibles. But he fought mightily to overcome those things, so he could fight the good fight on a larger stage, with a greater mission, and a deeper impact.

And so he was always on the move. Like the time when I spoke at a conference of newspaper editors. There was Cole, while everyone else was seated, walking slowly up the outside aisle of the room, only to stand at the bottom of the steps of the stage, so he could pounce when I finished. We hadn't met before, and he wanted to talk. He quickly pulled me into the empty ballroom next door to find a way to work together.

In that moment, in that vast empty ballroom, where just the two of us stood, I could feel the presence of a man who was on a mission, who held a deep affection for society and his profession, and who was willing to bring his full self to his efforts. I will remember that day forever.

Cole Campbell fought the good fight. His dogged pursuits were about people, their lives, and the relationship of his profession to them. This collection of his writings keeps his voice alive and helps guide us down a path of meaning and hope.

We are grateful, Cole.

A REMEMBRANCE

By Catherine L. Werner

OLE SPENT HIS LIFE pursuing and drawing out what he saw as truth, justice, and the greater good. Although he was raised Episcopalian and I Jewish, it was Cole who taught me about *tikkun olam*—the Hebrew phrase meaning "to heal the world," which, for him, was a way of being. Oftentimes that was reflected in his professional endeavors; always it was reflected in his personal relationships.  Cole was brilliant, insightful, and compassionate. Combined with his selfless willingness to serve as provocateur, Cole was able to influence many and achieve much during his too-short life. He identified often with Don Quixote; although at times on a seemingly futile quest, he never gave up pursuing his convictions.

Ever since he wrote a book on competitive debate in college, Cole had a dream of putting his professional thoughts into a book, so that others would be inspired to ponder, assess, react, or take the ideas further. I would like to thank the Kettering Foundation and its president, David Mathews, for seeing fit to publish this compilation reflecting some of Cole's thinking, as in doing so it fulfills one of Cole's greatest wishes. He would be so pleased if his musings served to provoke thought, foster dialogue, and encourage democratic deliberation. That is a legacy of which to be proud.

COLE C. CAMPBELL: AN APPRECIATION

By Tony Wharton

PEOPLE WHO HAD OCCASION to visit the spaces where Cole Campbell worked found themselves on the open range of Cole's intellect.

The signal feature of that landscape was books — piles of books on every imaginable subject, stacked not so tidily, on every surface. Each book bristled with slips of paper, bookmarks, sticky notes. While Cole read many books cover to cover, he hunted through countless others for insights, connections, hidden lights that reflected off another surface he hadn't seen, hadn't suspected. This rendered Cole's writing rich with layers of context and meaning as he drew upon a wide range of associations. In the articles and essays in this volume, Cole draws on Saul Bellow, Susan Sontag, Jedediah Purdy, Neil Postman, Taylor Branch, Toni Morrison, and Zen Buddhism, to name a very few influences.

I was fortunate to work with Cole for several years, first when he became editor of the *Virginian-Pilot* in Norfolk, Virginia. Technically, I worked *for* Cole, but it often didn't feel that way. Cole enlisted you to travel alongside him in an ongoing enterprise to see what you both could learn.

We might as well get out of the way now why you're reading these introductory notes, and why I'm writing them rather than Cole himself.

Cole's explorations were cut short in midwinter 2007. Driving to work in Reno, Nevada, he hit a patch of ice and skidded off the road. He was killed instantly.

His daughter, Claire, writes in a memorial essay:

> Work was always a central, energizing force in Dad's life; I don't think he saw it as "work" so much as an essential and rewarding entanglement with the world. . . . As I'm sure you all came to know firsthand, Dad always welcomed a challenge—not out of a former debater's desire to prove himself, but out of a deep conviction that what mattered was finding the best and most enlightened solution.

"Cole saw journalism's future, and I hate that he won't be lighting our way to the new world," said John Robinson, editor of the Greensboro *News and Record*, at Cole's memorial service.

> But I'm more interested today in talking about the Cole we all knew: his infectious humor, his over-the-top generosity; his flamboyant showmanship; his distinct ability to irritate the fool out of us. Ben Bowers once told me that when he wrote his memoirs, he was going to devote an entire chapter to Cole. I wouldn't frame it that way. To me, the Cole influence is more like a river that runs through it.

Cole was born in 1953 in Roanoke, Virginia, and was raised in Pulaski, a little town in the Appalachians. His father, John Robley Campbell, had been a lawyer, but became an Episcopal minister not long after Cole was born. His mother, Susie Clarke Campbell, was a psychology professor for 25 years. Teachers and writers peppered both sides of his lineage. Cole grew up, then, in a family that placed a high value both on learning and on service.

He was a middle child, with all the restless ambition that implies, and a Scot by heritage, so there was a healthy dose of stubbornness, too. At the University of North Carolina-Chapel Hill, he became a fierce, nationally recognized debater and wrote a book on competitive debate still cited in the field. All these qualities would become apparent in Cole's professional career, particularly when he engaged his whole mind and soul in what came to be known as "public journalism," a movement designed to reconnect journalism with democratic practices.

For Cole, who never stopped asking "why?," looking at the norms and values of journalism and asking whether they served a democratic purpose was inevitable. It was not so for many journalists. Although Cole rarely showed frustration, and would patiently explain his thinking to a skeptic time after time, I know it baffled him that many reporters and editors flatly refused to even entertain the questions he and others raised.

I learned so much from Cole in the years we worked together. I learned how thrilling experiments could be, when they succeeded and when they failed, even on the front pages of a widely read newspaper. I learned, too, what a powerful hold norms and routines have on professionals, and how those norms could be both satisfying and constrictive in the face of change.

Through persuasion, reasoning, and sly finesse, Cole persevered in his campaign against many of those norms through leadership positions at two newspapers and countless articles, speeches, and appearances on panels considering journalism and democracy. After he left the *St. Louis Post-Dispatch* in 2000, during stints at the Poynter Institute and the Kettering Foundation—when he began introducing himself as a "recovering journalist"—Cole began to look even more closely at the underpinnings of democracy, exploring the significance of community and citizenship in politics.

And even as he observed journalism from the outside, the field began changing ever more rapidly. The forces of connection, community formation, and self-publishing spawned by the Internet began to remake the landscape of journalism, as it did for business, politics, and most other fields. Suddenly, newspapers, which had scorned the notion of letting citizens into the newsroom, began frantically seeking new ways to connect with them. Most of these efforts were motivated more by survival instincts than by a reasoned consideration of journalism's place in a democracy, but they often arrived at the same place. As Donica Mensing and David Ryfe said in an assessment of Cole's impact:

> My, how times have changed. Just a decade later, Cole's great idea seems downright prescient. In the 1990s, journalists deeply resisted the notion of engaging their audiences in new ways. Today, "the people formerly known as the audience," to borrow a phrase from Dan Gilmor, often *are* the journalists.

Cole's career, however, moved fully into education. In 2004, he became dean of the Donald W. Reynolds School of Journalism at the University of Nevada, Reno, where he swiftly began integrating all he had learned about journalism, community, and democracy in a curriculum that would leave his imprint on the upcoming generation of journalists.

"We are undertaking an experiment in reconceiving journalism as a social practice, as a mediating institution in the generation of public knowledge," Cole wrote in an article for the Winter 2007 *Kettering Review* (which was published as a memorial issue to him). The Reynolds School, under his guidance, launched Our Tahoe, a project aimed at focusing both journalists' and citizens' attention on the issue of wildfire in the Tahoe basin. "All this experimentation is grounded on a detailed examination of current journalistic practice, and imagines new journalistic practices that better reflect what it takes for democracy to go well."

It was one of many, many experiments he had planned for the journalism school, ultimately for all of journalism.

Yet I would fail in my task if I let you think that journalism, democracy, and education constituted the whole of Cole's life and thought.

There's certainly enough there to occupy most people's lives. Not Cole's. At the time of his death he was writing a screenplay about college football, an intentionally subversive dictionary for journalists, and a book that would articulate his "unified theory," if you will, of journalism, community, and the need for social action. He wrote poetry, and love letters to his wife, Catherine. He took all the time he could spare from his work to spend with his infant son, Clarke. And he was constantly spinning out ideas—for books, for commercial ventures, for new creative endeavors.

E. Culpepper "Cully" Clark, dean of Grady College at the University of Georgia and a close friend of Cole's, said:

> Everything about Cole was a bit larger than life. His height, his stride, his eyes magnified by thick glasses, his whole physical presence was a vessel for that voice, a voice that could act, enfold, mesmerize, entertain, a voice so singular that there could be only one Cole. . . . More than anything else, he wanted to engage: engage your ideas, your interests, and yes, your passions.

That creative output is a double-edged sword, of course, for someone seeking to represent Cole in a setting such as this. There is so much material to choose from—yet so much remains achingly unfinished. Many of the projects he had underway were not in a form that could be published yet. A fragment of the dictionary is reprinted here, as well as all that he had written of the new book. I hope you come away from this volume inspired, as I am, by a man who poured such energy, passion, and critical thinking into everything he touched.

Tony Wharton is a journalist with 30 years' experience in newspapers and free-lance writing. He spent 12 years at the Virginian-Pilot *in Norfolk, Virginia, where he was part of Cole Campbell's team of public journalists. As an associate of the Kettering Foundation, he has edited several publications on journalism, government, and public dialogue. He lives with his family in Richmond, Virginia.*

MEANINGS OF PLACE;
PLACES OF MEANING

Cole wrote this personal essay as
part of the "Stalking the Spirit of Place"
seminar in 2001.

I N MY DREAMS there is a mountain. I get there by crossing a narrow
bridge over Peak Creek near my father's church in Pulaski, Virginia.
The road curves and rises through a valley crowded with shops and restaurants shoulder to shoulder like a medieval European city. I recognize
many favorites from my life in Chapel Hill. The thrill in stopping is picking a spot. The thrill in not stopping is reaching the mountain.

At the mountain's base are two paths. To the right, a footpath slides
under the green canopy and climbs the slope. The way is damp and cool,
with pine needles underfoot and oak leaves overhead. Leaves chant with
the wind's whisper. To the left, the road narrows and swings up and
around the mountain's flank, breaking out of tight bends onto broad vis-
tas of the valley below. The way is crisp and bright, with asphalt under
wheel and azure skies over sunroof. Sleeves dance with the wind's laugh-
ter. The mountaintop is like Table Rock, with fallen logs, thin trees, rocky
outcrops, a spring, and the occasional twig snap announcing unseen crit-
ters. The spring air and the spring water are clear.

I have made this trip, with different choices, many nights.

I was born in Roanoke, Virginia, in the Shenandoah Valley, and grew
up mostly in Pulaski, in the New River Valley, always surrounded by
the gentle Appalachians. Mountains are neighbors, home folk, kin. Nine-
tenths of my life has unfolded in Virginia and North Carolina, where all
of Gaia is divided into three parts: the mountains, the Piedmont, and the

coastal plain. A day's drive east or west covers the sweetest topography "under the cope of heaven."

I have lived midway between the Pacific Ocean and the San Francisco Bay. I have lived a block from a finger of the Elizabeth River that slips into Hampton Roads harbor that opens into the Chesapeake Bay that feeds the Atlantic Ocean. I have lived scant miles from the Mississippi River at mid-America. I now live 5 blocks from Lake Michigan and 45 minutes from creases of prairie. I have visited volcanoes on islands and tundra in the Arctic and tread lightly upon Asia and Europe and South America. All are beautiful. Mountains are neighbors, home folk, kin.

I am a Southerner and regard myself that way more often than I regard myself as a man or a Caucasian or a professional. Being a Southerner is being conscious of one's place, as defined by soil and by society.

By bloodlines, I am half Southerner and half Yankee—but still defined by my forebears' place of origin. My paternal grandmother was born and reared in Valparaiso, Indiana, where she bore my father, who grew up in Valparaiso, Chicago, and Glasgow, Virginia, his father's hometown, depending on where there was work during the Depression. My maternal grandfather moved from Ohio to Natural Bridge Station, Virginia, as a young man. He married a local girl from nearby Amherst County, known to the television age as the home of "Walton's Mountain."

I am not a Gothic Southerner, drunk on Faulkner and tipsy from Flannery O'Connor. But I have a Southerner's sensibility about place—that place is where people and nature create communities at once particular and universal. As Eudora Welty wrote: "It is through place that we put out roots, wherever birth, fate, chance, or our traveling selves set us down; but what these roots reach toward is the deep and running vein, eternal and consistent and everywhere purely itself."

Perhaps we Southerners love place all the more because it was in the South that war was first waged on place, not just on armies. General William Tecumseh Sherman brought total war to Georgia, just as General

Philip Sheridan brought total war to the valleys of Virginia. Homes and barns were torched, as were schools and stores. "Whatever one might say against General Sherman, one can say in his favor that he recognized the power and the significance of 'place,' " A. J. Conyers, a theologian at Baylor University, writes in *Modern Age* (Spring 2001). "And he was intent on leaving his enemies as few of those places as possible."

And still we wage war on place, with agricultural, industrial, commercial, and residential practices that scorch the earth with chemicals, monocultures, and bulldozer blades. And we sever our roots. And we unweave our communities.

There is no escaping responsibility for this, no mountaintop and no dreamscape secure from what must follow degradation of place, roots, community. There is work to be done. Wide awake.

ON WORK

M Y APPROACH to intellectual work is uncannily like the process described by C. Wright Mills in his essay, "On Intellectual Craftsmanship," which he included as an Appendix to his 1959 classic, *The Sociological Imagination.*

In the essay, Mills explains that the best social scientists do not separate work from life but meld experience with ideas. He said these scholars have an "ambiguous confidence," rely on conversations within a community of thinkers, look at issues from a host of disciplinary perspectives and—like journalists—value writing with clarity and voice as they reflect upon "the human variety."

He offers what I take to be the "three *R*'s" of intellectual work—reason, reading, and research ("empirical inquiry")—placing reason first among them. He encourages the serious scholar to keep "a special little file for his master agenda" for regular review and reshuffling, "one of the indispensable means by which your intellectual enterprise is kept oriented and under control." He cites constant sifting of ideas, searching for patterns, and building models and constructing charts, tables, and diagrams as "intellectual production" and "genuine tools of production." He reserves empirical inquiry, costly and troubling to manage, "to settle disagreements and doubts about facts, and thus to make arguments more fruitful by basing all sides more substantively. Facts discipline reason but reason is the advance guard in any field of learning."

Then, as I read this passage, it seemed as though the late professor had been tracking me from bookstore aisles to my cluttered study:

> After a few years of independent work, rather than read
> entire books, you will often read parts of many books from
> the point of view of some particular theme or topic in which
> you are interested and concerning which you have plans in
> your file. Therefore you will take notes, which do not fairly
> represent the books you read. You are using this particular
> idea, this particular fact, for the realization of your own
> projects.

If Mills were to visit my book-crammed spaces, or run into me in
the elevator hauling armloads of books from office to home, I would not
need to explain how I "read in" books so I can keep up with the seemingly unrelated accumulation driven by my current preoccupation. "You
do not really have to *study* a topic you are working on," he might say (as
he writes), "for as I have said, once you are into it, it is everywhere. You
are sensible to its themes; you see and hear them everywhere in your
experience, especially, it always seems to me, in apparently unrelated
areas."

While the body of *The Sociological Imagination* also would inspire
me, as I discuss below, Mills' jangled juxtaposition of understatement and
vaulting language resonates in the Appendix:

> Thinking is a struggle for order and at the same time for
> comprehensiveness. You must not stop thinking too soon—or
> you will fail to know all that you should; you cannot leave it to
> go on forever, or you yourself will burst. It is this dilemma, I
> suppose, that makes reflection, on those rare occasions when
> it is more or less successful, the most passionate endeavor of
> which the human being is capable.

Journalism as an intellectual craft

Last year, in a Crain Lecture Series presentation at Northwestern University, Tom Wicker of the *New York Times* said: "We need a print press

with an intellectual orientation, rather than focused on events and personalities. Is that kind of a press really possible in this country? I don't know, but I think we should find out. That's the only kind of print press that's going to survive."

Professor Paul Wang of Medill's Integrated Marketing Communications Department says that applied skills created the Gothic age of Western civilization, while conceptual skills gave us the Renaissance. With Mr. Wicker and Professor Wang, I also believe that journalism is an intellectual craft in need of a renaissance.

Most of our colleagues are intelligent men and women, some with Ivy League or graduate degrees, drawn to the work because it rewards brainpower. But many of them believe that journalism is inherently reflexive, not reflective. They pride themselves on their "news judgment," the wisdom (and power) accumulated like tree rings through years of instantaneous decisions. They reserve contemplation for sabbaticals, saying they have little other time for such luxury. They laud street smarts. They prefer categorical thinking—using traditional story lines, or *topoi*, to frame stories on the fly—to expansive thinking that leads to new categories and fresh perspectives. Like the French, they would rather starve their idiom than nourish it with concepts and terms borrowed from neighboring disciplines of inquiry and decision making.

I believe that many concepts currently embraced by journalists are necessary but not sufficient to the tasks facing us. Where some say journalism is essentially about distributing information and claiming attention, I say it must also be about increasing attentiveness. Where some say journalism must be interesting, important, and credible (as defined by journalists), I say it must also be meaningful and authentic (as defined by users).

Where some build protocols around finding and testing facts, I say we must also learn to find and test (usually tacit) frames. Where some seek accountability for the few, I say we must also pursue responsibility by the many. Where some focus on reality and irony, I say we must also focus on possibility and imagination. Where some say we must be detached observers, I say—echoing Gil Thelen of the *Tampa Tribune*—we must be committed observers.

Davis "Buzz" Merritt, former editor of the *Wichita Eagle*, has offered this instructive formulation: A successful community is one whose members know what is happening and take responsibility for it.

Traditional journalists understand the first criterion—knowing what's happening—in terms of standard reporting. But they don't quite fathom the second. An expanded conception suggests we journalists need to do more to help fulfill both criteria. We need to bulk up our capacity to help people know what is happening by honing our methods of inquiry and our models of how the world works. We need to help people move from a state of distraction and information overload to a state of attentiveness and mindfulness about truly important happenings. And, to help people take responsibility, we need to know more about social capital and civic engagement; adaptation; deliberation and choice work; cultural, community, and organizational learning and transformation; and related subjects.

I am interested in adaptation and how journalism contributes to its cognitive, emotional, and sociopolitical tasks—paying attention, working through knowledge, belief, and values, making choices. In a mouthful, my central professional interest is this: *How can journalism move from its current state—marked by economic uncertainty, professional anxiety, user dissatisfaction, and accelerated social transformation of the world it covers—to a future state in which journalists and their institutions are effective collaborators with citizens in building and sustaining successful communities?*

Conclusion

Toni Morrison says the real life of the book world is to allow people "to experience one's own mind dancing with another's." That's why I accumulate books—not as a bibliophile, but as someone who wants to keep his dance card full.

This reflects my desire to serve as a disciplined and thoughtful scholar-practitioner and student of democracy, public discourse, and public life. I plan to produce a body of intellectual work that will address the scholarly community, a body of professional work that will address the journalism community, and a body of general work that will address citizens and public communities. I want to reason, read, and research in all three domains. I want to publish in all three. I want to engage others, "to experience one's own mind dancing with another's," in all three.

I am much taken with this passage from Art Kleiner, coauthor of *The Fifth Discipline Fieldbook*, in a book he wrote about business management gurus:

> "New truths," said Thomas Huxley, "begin as heresies." He was defending Charles Darwin's theory of natural selection. He might have added that new heresies also begin as truths. A heretic is someone who sees a truth that contradicts the conventional wisdom of the institution—and remains loyal to both entities, to the institution and the new truth. Heretics are not apostates; they do not want to leave the "church." Instead, they want the church to change, to meet the truths that they have seen halfway.

I think journalism schools must blend keen insights into the best practices of the day as well as harbor heretics exploring new truths. My passion continues to be the cultivation of journalism as an intellectual enterprise.

AN INTERVIEW WITH COLE CAMPBELL

*On Oct. 3, 2003, New York University professor
Jay Rosen posted this interview with Cole on his
journalism-focused website, PressThink.*

Introduction—Jay Rosen: "Journalists act as if the world exists in one form only, which they discover each day and duly record for others to discover," says Cole Campbell, the former editor of the *St. Louis Post-Dispatch*, who often rejects standard "press think."

I have sometimes called the American press "a herd of independent minds." Cole Campbell has never been part of the herd, although he did run newsrooms as the top editor at the Norfolk *Virginian-Pilot* and the *St. Louis Post-Dispatch*. After 9/11, for example, he argued that journalists should "help citizens and communities, including political leaders, identify and respond to the most significant threats to well-being." Campbell is the coeditor with Roy Peter Clark of *The Values and Craft of American Journalism* (University Press of Florida, 2002). Here is our exchange:

Interviewer: *You have been an editor and writer in Chapel Hill, Raleigh, and Greensboro, North Carolina; Norfolk, Virginia; and St. Louis, Missouri. You have seen how journalists operate in these towns. You have also reflected on how journalists in each place think about their community. So is press think different in different places? Does it have a local identity?*

Cole Campbell: The Greensboro *News & Record* loves a well-written tale and has had many exceptional storytellers on its roster. The *News & Observer* in Raleigh finds its thrills in political intelligence and account-ability, while the *Chapel Hill News* exults in the intelligence of its college-town readership, community contributors, and staff. The *Virginian-Pilot* has a long tradition of overseas military coverage and in-depth explana-tory journalism. And the *St. Louis Post-Dispatch*, which brought us Tea-pot Dome and a third helping of the Pentagon Papers, looks high and low for official malfeasance.

But these papers are not, in the main, idiosyncratic. They are highly professional and highly professionalized. So key professional norms—autonomy, dramatizing stories through conflict, paying more attention to political front-runners in a crowded field of candidates, or presuming that newsmakers are authority figures rather than citizens—were evident in these newsrooms when I came to work in each. The Norfolk staff made a concerted effort to examine professional norms and developed a wider frame of reference than most newsrooms have.

Professional norms work well as day-in, day-out default positions. They are efficient means of organizing and executing deadline tasks. But when another idea might be called for, in such instances as cover-ing a 133-candidate field in the California recall campaign, falling back on these norms can lead to press think en masse. The trick, I think, is to embrace professional norms as useful, but recognize that they are fallible and contingent and need to be reviewed and recast. That, by the way, is a great function for journalism schools to perform.

Interviewer: *You said that journalists in all the cities where you worked saw newsmakers as authority figures rather than citizens. What is the chain of reasoning that lies behind this pattern?*

Cole Campbell: A team from the University of Missouri journalism school, led by Esther Thorson, conducted an audit of the *Post-Dispatch* in the late 1990s. One interesting finding was that the person least likely to be pictured in the paper was a woman over 50 (I think I am remembering the age correctly). Editors at the paper saw nothing unusual about that, saying that women over 50 are least likely to be newsmakers—elected or appointed officials, powerful business executives, or high-profile sports or entertainment figures.

By definition, then, news is not normally about people making their way through life, or working together to improve their communities, or acting as caregivers to others, or similar such activities in which citizens and neighbors take part. News is restricted to people with "power over" others rather than people who have "power with" others to get things done. I think this stems from the Enlightenment preoccupation with seeing power as dominance rather than seeing power also as capacity. And it's a useful way to reduce those to whom journalists must pay attention—people with official or celebrity standing.

Interviewer: *Can you tell me about someone in Raleigh or Norfolk or St. Louis who needed to be treated like a citizen, but instead was presumed an authority?*

Cole Campbell: Former Senator John Danforth is a key political, professional, and civic figure in St. Louis. He has headed up a regional visioning process called St. Louis 2004. That is a civic initiative calling upon the St. Louis business and professional community to contribute to the civic sphere, but its primary engagement with ordinary citizens has been to seek buy-in for its plans. If we could have gotten Danforth to see himself as a citizen and his initiative as an opportunity for other citizens to work together and think through St. Louis' immediate future, that would have been a major reframing that would have given citizens more control over their own destiny—which I think is the purpose of journalism. Many in the newsroom, however, viewed the 2004 initiative as just another special interest of the powers that be. They argued that if the paper paid too much attention to this initiative, we would be colluding with the power structure.

Interviewer: *You said, "If we could have gotten Danforth to see himself as a citizen." Who is the "we" that is active here?*

Cole Campbell: "We" refers to we, the journalists, engaging him. The best interviewers, I think, get their subjects to think about things in new ways, starting from new perspectives, so that the interviewees discover things about themselves or their situations or their tasks that they have not yet contemplated. If we had gotten Danforth to see himself as a citizen and talk about his work from that perspective, he might have discovered some truly interesting approaches. Or he might have offered some possibilities and dismissed them, for whatever reason. He would not lose control of his choices. We would only prompt him to offer more than reflexive responses.

Interviewer: *In your tour as newspaper editor, from North Carolina to Virginia to Missouri and around the profession, what is the one piece of press think you found hardest to counter, dislodge, or challenge?*

Cole Campbell: Most of my answer comes out of my tour of the profession outside of my own newsroom—in conference rooms, seminar rooms, and conventions. The most stubborn bit of press think is a myopic belief in realism as opposed to imagination. Journalists act as if the world exists in one form only, which they discover each day and duly record for others to discover.

In fact, the world that unfolds every day is shaped by people both acknowledging what is—realism—and imagining what might be. We journalists tend to discount people's efforts to envision what the world can become—until that vision is realized as an accomplished fact.

So we miss the opportunity to bear witness to the world becoming—or to help people guide more effectively what the world is becoming, rather than simply bemoan, begrudge, or otherwise react to what the world has become. In the same way, we tend to see our professional practices—and mind-sets—as the only practices and mind-sets, rather than reflecting on (imagining) how they might be improved.

Interviewer: *You have been out of daily journalism for several years now, working at the Poynter Institute. . . . Quite a change from the pressures of a newsroom. Distance is supposed to be an advantage, so when you look at daily journalism today, what do you notice about it that was not so apparent when you were meeting deadlines?*

Cole Campbell: My major epiphany may derive from being freed of deadlines, but I think it comes more from being freed of institutional identification with a particular source of news and information. I was aware of this as a working journalist, but I nonetheless discounted it in my daily routines.

My biggest realization has been how much people construct their own daily news reports, plucking from a variety of official news sources, such as newspapers or broadcast programs, as well as from a variety of websites (news-oriented and not-news-oriented) and especially from conversations, phone calls, and e-mails.

At the *Post-Dispatch* and the *Virginian-Pilot*, I acted on the assumption that the newspaper was the average person's sumptuous banquet of news and information. I knew people might pick up a taste of something else here and there from other sources, much the way a grocery shopper might stop at a gourmet shop for a specialty item not usually stocked at Kroger's or Publix. And both newsrooms collaborated with broadcasters and published online news. But we thought of our newspaper as clearly the main meal.

In my own news consumption now, I begin my day with news from the Web, which I check along with my e-mail before I've picked up the *Chicago Tribune* from my doorstep. Often the *Tribune*'s lead headline frames a topic I've read about 16 to 20 hours earlier on the Web in a way that suggests I surely must know nothing about it since I haven't gotten the *Tribune* until just now. During the invasion of Iraq, I skated across cable news channels, which are clustered on adjoining channels by my cable provider, never developing a favorite one because I was interested less in what their reporters or commentators had to say than in their photojournalism and whether Donald Rumsfeld was doing his daily dance with the press.

I get a handful of e-mail publications on health and economics. I listen to WBEZ (public radio) when I'm in my car. I return to the Web when I want to find a particular fact such as a sports score or an update on a player or coach. I get personal e-mails with hotlinks to interesting articles from people who are helping me edit the world of news and information, just like my mother used to send me clippings from my hometown paper (the *Winston-Salem Journal*). I talk to colleagues and cousins for the inside skinny on a variety of topics. I scan magazine racks for in-depth treatments on topics that capture my fancy and buy specialty journals or literary-style magazines when I want to focus on a subject.

Some of this is a daily ritual, but it is not a sophisticated effort at constructing Web filters and creating a Daily Me. It's much more like moving through the world and grazing on what this abundant infosphere offers, supplemented by very specific searches at very specific moments on very specific topics. I think newsrooms need to be thinking much more creatively about their place in an overall information ecology, rather than acting as though they are the information ecology.

I think newspapers might do well to reinvent themselves as print portals to a wide variety of news sources. The paper can position itself as a place to begin—or as a place to come back to—in seeing how all this news and information can be pieced together to create a coherent picture of the world. Right now, newspapers are a cacophonous assemblage of reports; they are not a coherent synthesis.

Interviewer: *Final question, Cole: recalling all the journalists you worked with as an editor, which book would you have them read to be better journalists, if you could have them all read and absorb the lessons of one book?*

Cole Campbell: My first impulse was to name John Hersey's *Hiroshima*, because it is a lovely fusion of craft and purpose. He uses a handful of Hiroshima survivors to weave multiple narratives on the aftermath of the atomic bombing. Beyond being a great read, the book is a classic of journalism as bearing witness, and it has an undeniably moral purpose—to help us know what happened and, by knowing, take some responsibility for it. My fear in recommending it is that it might be dismissed as the exception (I never get to write book-length journalism! I never cover historical events of this magnitude!) or admired only for its craft and not appreciated for its purpose.

So the book I'll recommend instead is Daniel Yankelovich's *Coming to Public Judgment*. It is not an example of journalism or about journalism (although Yankelovich writes about journalism in passing, and not fondly). It is about what David Mathews of the Kettering Foundation calls "public politics"—about how people work through what we journalists think of as issues in the news and how they come to public judgment about them (contrasted with the much more visible "public opinion"). If journalists read this book and work through its implications for their work, I think they could find ways to reinvigorate and transform journalism to make it of inestimable value to people struggling to understand, and shape, the world.

Journalism as a Democratic Art

Reprinted from The Idea of Public
Journalism, *edited by Theodore L. Glasser*
(Copyright Guilford Press, 1999
Reprinted with permission of the Guilford Press.)

W HEN PEOPLE COME TOGETHER to talk about their lives, their families, their neighborhoods, their communities, their cultures, their country, they repeatedly return to one pressing question.

We face all sorts of challenges, they say. What can we do—that works?

That question marks the intersection that ought to link citizens and professionals, journalists and academicians, doers, and thinkers.

Rarely do citizens, professionals, journalists, and academicians work together. Mostly, we stay within our own ranks. When we connect across the public domain, we often bring only part of what it takes to make a rich conversation.

Citizens may bring their demands, but not their hopes.

Professionals may bring their expertise, but not their vulnerability.

Journalists may bring their information, but not their ignorance.

Academicians may bring their critical acumen, but not their wonder.

Doers may bring their deeds, but not their failures.

Thinkers may bring their ideas, but not their imagination.

Demands, expertise, information, criticism, deeds, ideas—these are the grit of most public dialogue. Hopes, vulnerability, professed ignorance, wonder, failure, imagination—these are lost or derided or treated in passing.

The conversation is incomplete.

We face all these challenges. What can we do—together—that works?

How can we—as familiar strangers, as a democratic culture, as a political community—have better conversations?

This volume addresses these questions. What can citizens expect of professionals, journalists, and academicians? What can each of these practitioners expect of citizens? In particular, how can academicians—the authors of these chapters—collaborate more effectively with journalists—the object of these essays—in dealing with the challenges facing democracy, culture, community, and craft?

I come to this discussion as a journalist, as you can tell from my constricted idiom—shorter words, abrupt sentences, and paragraphs that fatten in 12-pica columns but flatten in this expanse of vellum.

We journalists have some beliefs that need reconsideration if we want to help our communities work through the problems confronting them. We believe, in the words of Alabama-born journalist William Bradford Huie, that we are in "the truth business." We believe that our product is information, offered up with a dash of entertainment. And we believe, as is noted elsewhere in this volume, that journalism has nothing to do with philosophy.

Having listened to citizens talk about their lives and their newspapers for more than 20 years, I've come to 3 different beliefs:

- Journalism is in the problem-solving business, not the truth business.

- Journalism's product is a contribution to understanding (but not a fully finished state of understanding). Therefore, journalism is as much about models for understanding the world as it is about information about the world.

- Journalism *is* philosophy—a philosophical construct of what is worth paying attention to and how best to pay attention to it.

Citizens want us to do a better job helping them and their communities address tough problems. They turn to us as one source, but not necessarily an exalted one, in piecing together their sense of the world. And they can see in what we publish and broadcast, despite our protestations that we only cover what's before us, that we have an underlying philosophy directing us to cast our coverage nets in one direction and not another.

Journalism is in disrepute because we are not living up to citizens' expectations. What would it be like if we took these ideas—journalism as problem solving, as contributing to understanding, and as a philosophy of attentiveness—seriously?

Journalism as problem solving

E. J. Dionne Jr. of the *Washington Post* calls on his colleagues to reconnect with citizens by focusing on the problems we all face:

> With the country passing through a series of crises, journalism's primary task ought to be to engage citizens in the quest for paths forward. That will involve understanding the alternatives and weighing them for their faithfulness not only to the facts but also to the values and moral commitments that supposedly underlie them. It involves debate experienced not simply as combat but also as conversation. In this telling, journalism's role of providing information is only the beginning of its task.

Too often, we journalists disavow any responsibility for our coverage. We pretend that news is a concrete thing that we merely collect and present, albeit with artful grace. We disavow any notion that we construct news by selecting which facts warrant attention and in what context. And we absolve ourselves further by saying our highest objective is the pursuit of truth. We are, in short, seekers of an already extant truth and we cannot be held accountable for merely sniffing it out.

And yet esteem for such truthhounds, in the eyes of the people we serve, continues to drop.

Philosopher Richard Rorty says that the highest aim of all forms of inquiry should not be truth. Truth is ineffable, Rorty says, ever receding before shifting definitions of what is true and shifting standards for testing truth. Instead, he argues, the highest aim of all inquiry should be problem solving, a far more practical and rewarding pursuit.

Even though Rorty makes his argument in the nearly ineffable language of academic philosophy, he speaks to the same imperative that Dionne addresses. And in a survey commissioned by the American Society of Newspaper Editors in 1997, citizens said they want newspapers to help them solve problems in their communities and to put energy into identifying solutions as well as problems. A 1994 survey by the *Times-Mirror* (now Pew) Center for the People and the Press, noted that nearly three-quarters of the respondents see the press as getting in the way of society solving its problems.

We journalists have a great opportunity if we make problem solving the raison d'être of our news report. That could recast how we cover everything, moving the discussion away from who wins or loses power to what problems we ought to solve and how we might tackle them. For example, rather than cover students' falling scores on standardized tests as an indictment of the current school administration, we could cover it as a problem to be solved by everyone with a stake in the issue—students, parents, teachers, neighbors, as well as school boards, superintendents, and principals. If any part of the community whose participation is crucial to the solution, including, but not limited to, the school administration, doesn't help develop and implement a solution, then we hold that part accountable.

Academicians can help us think through ways of identifying and describing problems and ways to help political players—citizens as well as official actors—solve them.

Journalism as contributing to understanding

In the 1960s and 1970s, scholars determined that the mass media couldn't tell people what to think but could tell people what to think about. Over the past decade, many scholars and practitioners have warned of the debilitating prospect of "information overload," "information anxiety," "the information explosion," and the like.

Edward O. Wilson, the Harvard sociobiologist, projects into the next millennium:

> In the 21st century, the world will not be run by those who possess mere information alone. Thanks to science and technology, access to factual knowledge of all kinds is rising exponentially while dropping in unit cost. It is destined to become global and democratic. Soon it will be available everywhere on television and computer screens. What then? The answer is clear: synthesis. We are drowning in information, while starving for wisdom. The world henceforth will be run by synthesizers, people able to put together the right information at the right time, think critically about it, and make important choices wisely.

Will we journalists merely swamp people with information, or will we help people achieve synthesis? If we want the world to be run by democrats in the next millennium, shouldn't as many people as possible master the skills of synthesis? How can news media as mass media help secure that mastery?

Merely pumping more information through the fire hoses of news reports, or aiming those fire hoses at more issues, does not lead to synthesis. People also need more useful ways of processing the information. Journalists, working with academicians, can give people better models and tools.

Alfred R. Oxenfeldt, professor emeritus of business at Columbia University, writes:

Few of the models governing our actions are based on careful study and reflection. As a result, they are likely to be only partially correct and could be seriously flawed. Faulty beliefs, both conscious and unconscious, rather than limited information, explain most poor decisions and misguided actions.

Flawed models and faulty beliefs, not limited information. Oxenfeldt continues:

Valid models are extremely valuable intellectual tools. They convey and embody basic understanding of, and insight into, complicated phenomena. Such understanding enables executives to know what information to collect and how to interpret it. Facts alone usually are ambiguous and bewildering.

Substitute for *executives* any of those we are talking about—citizens, professionals, journalists, academicians—and the conclusion holds up.

We need to reexamine many of our existing models of how the world works, which, as deadlines loom, we reflexively use to funnel new facts into old wineskins. Mark Silk of the *Atlanta Journal-Constitution* reminds us that ancient Greek rhetoricians called these devices *konoi topoi*, or "commonplaces." He cites a list of "Basic Religion Stories" compiled by Peter Steinfels of the *New York Times*:

- Religious leader reveals feet of clay (or turns out to be scoundrel)

- Ancient faith struggles to adjust to modern times

- Scholars challenge long-standing beliefs

- Interfaith harmony overcomes inherited enmity

- New translation of sacred scripture sounds funny

- Devoted members of a zealous religious group turn out to be warm, ordinary folks

Any careful reader can spin out similar topoi for all kinds of news coverage: the indefatigable entrepreneur who beats the conglomerate at its own game, the fearsome athlete/rock star/police officer who volunteers to work with disadvantaged children, the public official who—can you believe it—really means what she says.

Unfortunately, stories that don't fit these commonplace models often don't get covered. And many journalistic topoi in fact don't describe reality. Scholar after scholar has documented journalists' proclivity to rely on set story lines that don't fit the facts. Political scientist Thomas E. Patterson challenges the journalistic topoi that presidents' campaign promises are smokescreens for their real intentions. He documents that presidents pursue almost all of their campaign promises while the news media fixate on the few deviations, which may be driven by any number of factors beyond sneakiness. Historian David Thelen challenges the topoi of Olliemania[1] by contrasting news coverage of the Iran-Contra hearings with citizens' correspondence to the House committee holding the hearings.

It's time to reexamine lots of basic models that journalists employ. Among them:

- The model that power corrupts and therefore must always be constrained. Under what circumstances should power be increased? In 1925, Mary Parker Follett argued that "genuine power is capacity" and in the 1990s, Jay Rosen and others have argued that the press could play a role in increasing the capacity of citizens and communities to act to solve the problems facing them.

- The model that conflict is a win-lose proposition and best seen through a juxtaposition of extremes. Follett and others note that there are lots of ways conflict can be resolved to satisfy the interests of all parties, while Richard Harwood and others argue that it helps to attend to the tensions that underlie staked-out positions. And they argue that most people aren't at the extremes on any issue.

---

[1] Oliver North was at the center of the Iran-Contra scandal of the 1980s.

Instead, they are distributed along a continuum of positions, or they are ambivalent rather than resolved about where they stand.

- The marketplace model, used to explain all kinds of noneconomic activity, including elections, and blamed for all kinds of problems in journalism itself. (It's easier to blame capitalists and bosses than to reexamine the routines of thought we all use; on the other hand, as a journalist, I can change the way I think and act more easily than I can restructure the media economy.) What if we conceived of elections not as a swap of promises for votes but as a time for performance appraisals of incumbents and a job selection process for all aspirants to office? These metaphorical constructs are just as accurate and give new dimensions to coverage.

Jay Rosen, Richard Harwood, and others already have developed some new tools for journalists to use, including the constructs of *framing stories*, incorporating within the frame possible ways of responding to a problem, *positioning citizens* as political actors and not just as spectators, and *mapping* ways to tap into layers of knowledge within communities. Journalists around the country are experimenting with other tools, from community conversations to deliberative polling to more sophisticated open-ended interviewing techniques. (Some, as advocated elsewhere in this volume, are even using coupons to engage citizens.) Others are exploring tools to measure and report on the health of their communities along a number of dimensions: physical, social, civic, and political.

These tools are more than epistemological devices. They are also means of sorting for relevance and meaning, of helping citizens engage more effectively in public life so that they can more effectively synthesize information and, in Wilson's phrase, "make important choices wisely." Over time, some tools may prove as durable and long lasting as a handsaw, whereas others will appear as curious and marginal as kitchen gimmick-gadgets touted in midnight television commercials.

But we should proceed in moving toward the "understanding" or "meaning" business with humility. Richard Harwood and his colleagues at the Harwood Group, which specializes in studying the public realm, have documented the fact that citizens don't turn to the news media for understanding per se, but for input. They place journalistic input alongside their own life experience and input from families, friends, coworkers, and neighbors. They sort through all this to come to an understanding of the world, to complete their own acts of synthesis.

In that sense, they see journalism as a raw material, or a refined commodity, more than as a finished, complete product. If we strengthen the models we use to describe the world, and give citizens better tools, we may increase our value. But we should recognize that we will always be contributors to understanding and never providers of it.

Journalism as a philosophy of attentiveness

Saul Bellow, novelist and Nobel laureate, is the kind of person we'd like to think loves newspapers—given our self-image as windows to the world, mirrors of society, defenders of free expression. If that's what we thought, we would be wrong, as Bellow made clear in "The Distracted Public," a 1990 address at Oxford University. He estimates that an average weekday *New York Times* contains more information than an Elizabethan would have acquired in a lifetime. "What good is such a plethora of information?" he asks. "It simply poisons us." He continues:

> Newspapers must be read cautiously, cannily, defensively. You know very well that journalists cannot afford to tell you plainly what is going on. There are dependable observers who believe that the press cannot give Americans anything like a true picture of the world. The written word is untrustworthy and the spoken word (radio and TV) irresponsible. . . . The government does not seem able to understand or to explain its authority, the grounds for its decisions. Its antagonist, the press, interprets the government's operations in such a way as to destabilize

29

public judgment. The jargon used by both antagonists excites, it thrills, it bewilders, it frightens, it confuses, it annihilates coherence, it makes comprehension utterly impossible....

Of course, the ceaseless world crisis, otherwise known as the chaos of the present age, is not the work of the communications industry and its Information Revolution; but for our peculiar pseudoknowledge of what is happening, for the density of our ignorance, and for the inner confusion and centerlessness of our understanding, for our agitation, the communicators are responsible. Intellectuals and universities, from the ideological side, also have much to answer for.

Bellow's solution: "Writers, poets, painters, musicians, philosophers, political thinkers, to name only a few of the categories affected, must woo their readers, viewers, listeners, from distraction." A novelist who demonstrates "a distinct and human quality . . . more musical than verbal," he says, "has power over distraction and fragmentation, and out of distressing unrest, even from the edge of chaos, he can bring unity and carry us into a state of intransitive attention. People hunger for this."

Too often, journalism settles for distraction, whether labeled celebrity news, entertainment, sensationalism, or "tabloidization of the news." If we cast journalism as a philosophy of attentiveness—a system of thinking about what to pay attention to and how to pay attention—we begin to see its real, enduring value. Our main contribution is not information or understanding but a kind of ordering of topics worthy of contemplation, conversation, and further inquiry.

Ronald A. Heifetz has put forward a new model of leadership, and a systematic explanation of how it works, that centers on adaptive change. His model begins with, and frequently returns to, paying attention. Journalists could model much of what we do around it.

Heifetz contrasts the notion that "leadership means influencing the community to follow the leader's vision" with "leadership means influencing the community to face its problems." Effective leaders do the latter, he says. Specifically, effective leaders do the following:

- Direct attention. "Getting people to pay attention to tough issues rather than diversions is at the heart of strategy."

- Test reality. "Because authorities are expected to know, they are given *access to information*. . . . Authority figures are supposed to be agents of reality testing: they are supposed to investigate problems more objectively than people in the problems' grasp. By virtue of their authority, they are given a special *vantage point* from which to survey and understand the situation. They can compare different sources of evidence." (Emphasis in the original.)

- Manage information and frame issues. "People are more likely to pay attention to arguments and perspectives about which they feel some urgency. Urgency, well framed, promotes adaptive work." If only a few see an important issue as urgent, "the strategic challenge will be to find ways to generate more generalized urgency, and thus ripen the issue."

- Orchestrate conflicting perspectives. "Pieces of the puzzle—information about the problem—lie scattered in the hands of stakeholders across divisions, interest groups, organizations, and communities. Not only is the information scattered, but the solution requires adjustments in the attitudes and behaviors of many people across boundaries. Hence, an authority who excludes stakeholders from defining and solving the problem risks developing an incomplete solution or a solution to the wrong problem."

- Choose the decision-making process. "Adaptive situations . . . tend to demand a more participative mode of operating to shift responsibility to the primary stakeholders. Because the problems lie largely in their attitudes, values, habits, or current relationships, the problem solving has to take place in their hearts and minds. One produces progress on adaptive problems by working the conflicts within and between the parties."

This is an equally powerful blueprint for effective journalism. We don't want to influence citizens to follow our vision of what ought to be done. We do want to influence citizens to face their own problems by helping them identify and rank them. (Why else are we writing about them?) Paralleling effective leaders, effective journalists do these things:

- Direct attention—by bearing witness to what matters most: the great themes of life and the great issues of the day, as well as the daily urgencies and insurgencies that shape the worlds of the people and communities we serve.

- Test reality—by the same process available to leaders: access to information and a vantage point free of self-interest, open to weighing various sources of information.

- Manage information and frame issues—to make them urgent and ripe for discussion. We call these "news pegs" and "nut grafs," designed to explain why an issue needs attention now.

- Air conflicting perspectives—moving beyond both-sides-of-the-story narrowness to a wide-ranging exploration that helps citizens understand not only their own stake in an issue but also the stakes of others.

- Describe the decision-making process—and hold all parties (including citizens, as political actors and not passive spectators) accountable for their part in it.

In this model, neither leaders nor journalists take away power or responsibility from the community. Rather, they help order the discussion to ensure that communities face their problems.

This is a pragmatic process by which we journalists can give life to our philosophy of attentiveness. This can be our contribution to the rich philosophy of public life as communication, as conversation, put forward by John Dewey in the 1920s, enriched by James Carey and Jay Rosen in recent years, and described and critiqued in this volume.

Journalism as fact-finding, storytelling, and conversation-keeping

Over the years, I have come to appreciate two traditions of journalism: fact-finding and storytelling. The fact-finding tradition treats citizens as clients and helps create something akin to what John Dewey called "pragmatic intelligence." Its most energetic expression has been muckraking, investigative journalism, and explanatory journalism; its weakest is what Ross Perot popularized as "gotcha journalism." The storytelling tradition treats citizens as an audience and, through something akin to what Gerald Early calls "the power of aesthetic experience," delivers epiphanies of understanding or emotional catharsis. Its most energetic expression has been human-interest journalism, New Journalism, and literary journalism. Its weakest expression is gossip mongering and celebrity obsession.

Only by paying attention to the philosophical drivetrain of Dewey-Carey-Rosen have I come to recognize and appreciate a third tradition—the conversation-keeping tradition. The conversation-keeping tradition treats citizens as partners and helps them be part of something akin to what Ralph Ellison called "the reflective consciousness" of our culture. Its most energetic expression has been the synergy between print and talk that has characterized the expansion of democracy to ever-widening circles of Americans.

Historian Robert H. Wiebe writes that the extraordinary energy needed to sustain and transform democracy in the early 19th century was produced by a blend of newspaper reading and conversation. The emerging network of newspapers inspired citizens—restricted then, in terms of full voting rights, to white male adults—to make themselves literate in order to stay connected to public debate. Norms for public discussion changed, creating "a lightly polished everyday language" that "served nationally as a medium for democratic discussion."

Participation, Wiebe writes, was the essence of democracy:

> Democratic politics was a vibrant public process: marching, chanting, disputing, debating, voting. People entered this process by demanding a place. The anger at secrecy, the demand for openness, was a functional response to situations that made democracy impossible. Without access, citizens have no role; private dealings paralyzed them. . . . The fact that citizens were "perpetually acting" in public life did not, as several Europeans suggested, signal a nationwide nervous disorder. Americans were keeping their democracy alive. At rest everything disappeared.

Unfortunately, in the early 20th century, journalists changed sides. We took to heart the world view of Walter Lippmann, whose book, *Public Opinion*, James Carey calls "the founding book of modern American journalism." Carey summarizes Lippmann's view, and the current practice of our craft:

> Journalists primarily served as conduits relaying truth arrived at elsewhere, by the experts—scientists in their laboratories, bureaucrats in their bureaus. The truth was not a product of the conversation or debate of the public or the investigations of journalists. Journalists merely translate the arcane language of experts into a publicly accessible language for the masses.

Lippmann saw a need for "the hot light of publicity," which kept the experts from being "altogether ruthless." The problem, Carey argues, is that this "democratic politics of publicity and experts . . . confirmed the psychological incompetence of people to participate in it. Again, it evolved a political system of democracy without citizens."

As a result, Carey concludes, we have a debased journalism:

> We developed a journalism that was an early-warning system but one that kept the public in a constant state of agitation or

boredom. It is a journalism that reports a continuing stream of expert opinion, but because there is no agreement among experts it is more like observing talk-show gossip and petty manipulation than like bearing witness to the truth. It is a journalism of fact without regard to understanding through which the public is immobilized and demobilized and merely ratifies the judgments of experts delivered from on high. It is, above all, a journalism that justifies itself in the public's name but in which the public plays no role, except as an audience; it is a receptacle to be informed by the experts and an excuse for the practice of publicity.

The fights between the press and its sources are mostly over sources erecting "ever more complicated veils of appearance over events" and journalists trying "ever more assiduously to pierce the veil." The public has become increasingly bored, alienated, and cynical, "learning to distrust appearances mounted by both elites and journalists and, most damagingly, to distrust all language, to look at language as a mere instrument of interest and obfuscation." The result:

> Today, Americans have lost interest in politics. . . . Above all, the press lost credibility and respect; it was no longer believed. As poll after poll showed, journalists had earned the distrust of the public and were increasingly seen as a hindrance to, rather than an avenue of, politics and political reform.

If we don't want to further debase democracy, we need to reinvigorate journalism's conversation-keeping tradition. We journalists can contribute ideas and information to that conversation, but mostly we must heed what ordinary citizens are saying, invite them back into the political dialogue we cover and reflect that in our newspapers and broadcasts. We can help order the flow of what's worth discussing immediately and what might wait for another day, as long as we see ourselves as partners with, and not cleverer than, the people and communities we serve.

What do we do now?

There is much that we as journalists and academicians can work on to increase our own effectiveness and contribute to increasing citizens' and professionals' effectiveness. Academicians must help create new models and tools, not merely critique them, because these models and tools need to be alloys of practice and theory, ideas and action.

Here's a beginning list of things we need to do:

- Write more expressively about public life, using the experiences and aspirations of citizens less as illustrative anecdotes and more as compelling narratives.

- Learn more about the process of problem solving, so we can fashion more helpful news reports that address problems and devising solutions to them.

- Create new models and tools for our own work and for citizens and professionals to use in their work.

- Learn more about attentiveness from all the disciplines of attention, whether cognitive psychology or Zen Buddhism.

- Incorporate the lessons of adaptive change in the way we frame news reports, to help keep pressure on political communities and political actors (including citizens) to work through the problems confronting them.

- Widen and deepen our understanding of dialogue, deliberation, and conversation, so that our journalism can better reflect it, contribute to it, and, as appropriate, help order it. We need to include the emotional and intuitive components of conversation, as well as the rational elements.

- Recognize that public life is expressed not only through public discourse but also through public work—when citizens come together to create real and lasting institutions. We can cover this better, as well.

- Bring newsrooms into universities and universities into newsrooms, to increase collaboration and learning on both sides.

• Strengthen and integrate the three traditions of fact-finding, storytelling, and conversation-keeping.

There is also revolutionary work to be done, if we dare. Here are two ways we could radically transform our journalism—as journalists:

What if we reoriented our journalism away from the sources of news and toward the recipients of news? Instead of building our beats around institutions and agencies, what if we built them around the troubles and joys in people's lives? Instead of a City Hall beat, we might have a political participation beat that tracks what's happening at City Hall in a way that helps citizens directly influence it. Instead of covering doctors and medical breakthroughs using patients as illustrations of what health-care professionals can accomplish, suppose we covered patients and used doctors and medical breakthroughs as illustrations of problem solving. What if we thought of institutions and agencies not as *sources of news* but as *resources for problem solving* that citizens could tap and work with?

What if we reoriented our journalism away from description of the present and toward imagination of a better alternative? Maxine Greene, an education professor at Columbia University, has come to "concentrate on imagination as a means through which we can assemble a coherent world" in part because "imagination is what, above all else, makes empathy possible. It is what enables us to cross the empty spaces between ourselves and those we teachers have called 'other' over the years . . . of all our cognitive capacities, imagination is the one that permits us to give credence to alternative realities." She goes further:

> We also have our social imagination: the capacity to invent visions of what should be and what might be in our deficient society, on the streets where we live, in our schools. As I write of social imagination, I am reminded of Jean-Paul Sartre's declaration that "it is on the day that we can conceive of a different state of affairs that a new light falls on our troubles and our

suffering and that we decide that these are unbearable." That is, we acknowledge the harshness of situations only when we have in mind another state of affairs in which things would be better. . . . And it may be only then that we are moved to choose to repair or to renew.

We cannot give up description of the present; it is essential to directing attention, testing reality, and framing issues. But we should not let it dominate our mind-set and our typeset and our studio sets. We should make equal room for conceiving of alternative ways of living in a just world.

In offering these more radical ideas, I am mainly calling on us to continue the experimentation this volume discusses in detail. It is true to our democratic history, in which little is fixed and everything seems always at risk. As Jean Bethke Elshtain has written:

> From Jefferson's bold throwing down of the gauntlet to the British Empire, not knowing whether the upshot would be "hanging together or hanged separately," to Lincoln's "nation so conceived and so dedicated," to Martin Luther King's dream of an essentially pacific democratic people who judge their fellow citizens by the content of their character not the color of their skins, democratic culture has been a *wager*, not a frozen accomplishment.

Our job as journalists and academicians, as citizens and professionals, is to keep anteing up—and to keep democratic culture a worthy bet. That's the culture I want to pass on, reenergized, to the next generations. We must perpetually act to keep democracy alive. At rest, everything disappears.

"Cash-Cow" Journalism and the Sigmoid Curve

*Unlike many journalists who preferred not to
think about the business side of journalism
(until very lately, perhaps), Cole knew his history,
and he appreciated the significance of the relationship
between the newsroom and the "suits." This essay,
apparently intended for a public-speaking occasion,
argued—presciently—that journalists ignored
such forces at their peril.*

THE WORLD OF JOURNALISM is marked by great tension between boardrooms and newsrooms, between those who count the beans and those who spill them. This tension reflects bona fide economic anxiety. We work in a time of economic transformation—and disruption—that is as vast as the global economy and as near at hand as the particular newspaper, broadcast station, cable channel, or online venture we serve. Amid this turbulence, we ponder how we can continue to reward both those who do quality journalism and those who invest in it. And we wonder: How much reward is enough?

In essence, we are trying to leap between two curves of the business life cycle. Traditional print and broadcast vehicles are considered economically mature, while our online and multimedia vehicles are red-ink startups. Successful startups move through a growth phase to become "cash cows" that produce substantial profits for dividends and for investment—in continued growth or in new products or businesses. Once a cash cow has passed its growth peak, it becomes a prime target for what consultants at McKinsey & Co. euphemistically call "harvest" strategies: Owners stop investing and instead manage the operation to harvest whatever economic value is left.

Economists plot business life cycles on a slanted, elongated *S* called "the sigmoid curve." Many of our companies are trying to jump from the top hook of a mature sigmoid curve, before its downward turn plummets, to the bottom hook of a new curve that promises to skyrocket. And so we are engaged in much chin scratching about what kinds of journalism, journalistic vehicles, and journalistic business models will work in the future.

Our newsrooms are located at the confounding intersection of what we are willing to sell—news products to our audiences, audiences and editorial settings to our advertisers—and what we *are not* willing to sell—the pursuit of truth, the free expression of ideas, our disinterested professional judgment. We proclaim that our newsrooms are repositories walled off from commerce, and then we charge them with developing news reports that are engaging enough (or efficient enough) to warrant the time our customers invest in them—in other words, packages of truth, free expression, and professional judgment that are marketable.

We journalists are disoriented in a world in which everything is assessed in terms of its exchange value—can it attract new readers, new advertising dollars, new profits? "Often enough, money fails to represent value," philosopher Michael Walzer of Princeton University says. "The translations are made, but as with good poetry, something is lost in the process."

So of course we are tense.

To reduce our sense of vulnerability, we now clad ourselves in the chain mail of values. We espouse several values, including accuracy, fairness, and truth telling. But every day we acknowledge falling short of our ideals because of the crush of deadlines, the overload of information, the unreliability of sources. Yet we never let such circumstances compromise our most cherished professional ideal—our autonomy. We believe that autonomy is our only guarantor of accuracy, fairness, truth telling, etc. We protect it at all cost. We call the shots on what constitutes news, acceptable journalistic performance, sound professional judgment. Period.

Disinterested, independent judgment is crucially important. But in too many newsrooms, we have exaggerated our notion of autonomy to the point that we deride learning from people who are not journalists, including citizens, experts in other fields, and our colleagues from other departments.

The Readership Initiative undertaken by Northwestern's Media Management Center has documented that newspapers have defensive cultures, marked by what it calls perfectionism and oppositional styles. Specifically, we lose sight of overall goals, get lost in details, coordinate little with others, and have unproductive conflicts that result in safe but ineffectual decisions. This is a far cry from the constructive learning cultures needed to thrive in an intensely competitive, ever-changing world.

Newsrooms are particularly resistant to three key elements of a market orientation: being committed to gathering market intelligence, sharing market intelligence internally, and coordinating among departments.

We don't protect our independence by rejecting the counsel or input of our readers, viewers, listeners, or browsers, and we don't give it up by seeking that input. We assert our independence in deciding how to respond. We must exercise independent judgment—but not until we have gotten the information we need (in fact, depend on) from our sources, our colleagues, and our users.

When the talk turns to business, we journalists often talk about the Wall and the Slippery Slope—moral topography that places us as defenders of the inner sanctum and the high ground. And it places our non-journalist colleagues as barbarians at the gate or denizens of the murky depths. When we invoke this imagery, we not only give offense, we also wall ourselves off from our principal (and principled) allies in building strong journalistic franchises—those who lead the rest of the enterprise.

It's all right if we have different opinions and different interests. Conflict within constructive cultures (not defensive ones) is a great source of creative breakthroughs. In robust discussions of what matters, what thrills us, what scares us, the best arguments should prove their worth—even when immediate interests diverge. Our long-term interests are the same—good journalism that sustains good business, good business that sustains good journalism.

We might do well to reorient our values discussion away from defensive crouching and toward catalyzing change. In *Built to Last*, James C. Collins and Jerry Porras studied 18 gold-medal companies whose stock valuation has increased more than 5 times the marketplace average across nearly a century. What do these companies share? All have an enduring purpose and sustaining values that shape their decisions and align their operations. Their purpose and their values never change, but everything else in these companies can—to ensure that the companies pursue their purpose and values even as markets change, technologies change, regulations change, customers change, competitors change.

Too often in news organizations, we see innovation as a threat rather than as a means to revitalize our organizations and thus conserve our values. We treasure what we already know and devalue what we don't. If we insist on self-enclosed cultures that inflate autonomy and deride learning, no values discussion can save us. Undercovered and alienated communities will remain undercovered—and alienated. The perception gap between citizens and journalists over whether we journalists adhere to our shared values will widen. Our relevance—and our audience's attention to us—will continue to decline.

In his 1974 classic, *Beyond the Front Page*, Chris Argyris of Harvard links newsrooms' "self-sealing, non-learning processes that lead to organizational dry rot" with "the credibility gap that exists between newspapers and the public."

"The genuine autonomy of newspapers therefore may depend ultimately upon their being able to manage themselves," he writes.

> But in order to accomplish this objective, newspapers will have to find ways to reduce the repetitive, compulsive processes of their internal systems. A system that behaves compulsively in ways that its members acknowledge are ineffective creates the conditions for organizational neurosis and invites outside intervention and control.

Consider the fate of the *Los Angeles Times*. The *Times*' owners lost patience because insiders had not fixed long-standing problems—inefficient use of resources, the neglect of Latino readers, a weak profit-and-loss statement. So the owners brought in outsiders with no journalism experience to run the company. On their watch, The *Times* Sunday magazine shared revenues from a special edition with the edition's subject—the new Staples Center. The outsiders didn't see the problem—until the subsequent outcry that led ultimately to the sale of the company and their ouster. The outsiders lost their way, but—in a different dimension—so had the insiders before them.

We cannot ignore the requirements—or the values—of either good journalism or good business. If we do, those who can hold us accountable—our employers, our customers—will start looking for others who can attend to both.

DICTIONARY FOR JOURNALISTS—AND THOSE WHO PAY ATTENTION TO THEM

One of Cole's many unfinished projects was a "dictionary" for journalists. The concept was simple— redefine the standard lingo of journalism from the perspective of public journalism. Its goal was far more ambitious: compelling journalists to think about the words they use everyday and the ideas behind them.

I LOVE REAL DICTIONARIES for their wisdom and their fussiness and their heft. I particularly like big, fat volumes that tell you the history, lineage, and genealogy of words—including words like *lineage* and *genealogy*. I have bought a lot of dictionaries over the years and occasionally use one.

Ambrose Bierce notwithstanding, I am not a big fan of the dictionary format as a way to write about something beyond definitions and etymology. I prefer books with sweeping narratives, well-ordered outlines, or spiffy graphics that carry forward the main line of argument. Faux dictionaries that offer analysis in the guise of definitions generally strike me as formulaic, strained, and too chopped up to be coherent.

I am writing this dictionary in part as a distraction from everything else I'm working on, in part as an experiment in writing: Can I just sit down and hammer out some thoughts without a grand outline, tapping everything I've been fretting about in three decades as a practitioner of journalism? Can I write in a conversational voice, indulge in personal inflection, and still communicate some serious ideas?

And I am writing this dictionary because the struggle to reinvent, rejuvenate, renew, restore, reform, and otherwise reshape journalism to keep it vital keeps foundering on fundamental questions, ill-defined terms, and unacknowledged and unanalyzed models of the way the world works.

I wasn't contemplating writing a dictionary when I started listing a handful of terms that I think are particularly misunderstood or misapplied or dealt with in such telegraphic shorthand as to be meaningless— terms such as *accountability*, *credibility*, *democracy*, and *excellence*. But the list kept growing as I thought about significant terms and nuances that journalists don't deal with much. The list now includes some terms quite familiar to journalists and scholars or users of journalism as descriptors of journalistic practice, such as *analysis*, *credibility*, *daily*, and *fact*. It includes terms that describe journalistic processes or outcomes, such as *accountability*, *attention*, *craft*, *diversity*, *events*. And there are some terms that come from the universe of writing—*author*, *authorial voice*, *fiction*—that do not belong exclusively to journalism.

For the most part, this is a dictionary of terms journalists don't normally use. Roy Peter Clark of the Poynter Institute for Media Studies has written a brilliant paper on why journalists abjure certain words. And we certainly should disdain language that is vague or misleading in crafting our work. In fact, ideology and pronouncements aside, far too many journalists get caught up in the technical language of their sources, from police to scientists to—worst offenders of all—educational administrators. So news stories are filled with references to "apprehending and transporting suspects," "verifiable outcomes," and similar opacity. And newsrooms are filled with an officially sanctioned idiom that corrupts the spelling or meaning of ordinary words in a fashion impenetrable to civilians—and sometimes even to journalists from other newsrooms:

lede, graf, head, jump, turn, bishop, cut, V.O., splice, B-copy (or is *A-copy* preferred here?).

But we journalists can learn a lot by broadening and deepening our vocabulary. Words that originate outside the journalistic argot can help us think in new ways about how to make our craft more compelling and meaningful to those who use us. Journalists who insist on keeping journalese "pure" remind me of the French. A century ago, Great Britain dominated the globe militarily and economically, but French was the lingua franca, the world's language. Now the United States dominates the globe, and English is the new lingua franca. The difference is not between French and American influence, but in the acceleration of change across the globe and the need for an elastic language that can communicate new ideas and experiences. French, having been kept pure, contains about 100,000 words, whereas English now includes 500,000-plus general terms and another 500,000-plus technical terms.

Where does English get its new words? From other languages, from sheer fantasy, from crashing words into each other like atoms to create new molecules. Journalists who want to adapt to new circumstances in the world we cover and the newsrooms we inhabit may need some new terms. We certainly can use some new words to understand, and in some cases reimagine, what we do, how we do it, and why it matters.

This dictionary is a compilation of some of those words. Like a real dictionary, this one will offer definitions. Sometimes this dictionary will offer casual etymology, or at least the source from which I learned a term if I can remember it. Most definitions will be serious, but some will be a tad satirical to make a larger point. I hope the serious and the satirical will be self-evident. If not, here's a clue: The shorter the entry, the more likely it's included for comic relief or sardonic commentary.

This is a first-person dictionary, but only mildly so. I will speak occasionally in the first-person singular and first-person plural. The "we" in these cases mostly will be a syncopation of "we journalists." Sometimes the context might be about "we citizens."

This dictionary is not intended exclusively for journalists. I hope it appeals to those of you who study, use, or think about journalism. In a democratic society, we journalists hope or presume that includes everybody. But there is much evidence to suggest you are a more selective lot. Several entries will discuss, if not literally define, this circumstance and suggest new ways—new terms, if you will—to deal with it.

[A few excerpts from the dictionary follow—ed.]

Amass—What media owners attempt to do to wealth.

Change—A curse word. An inevitable state of being.

Elections—Focal point of political journalism; secular high holiday of the newsroom.

Love—We journalists are quite comfortable talking about whether we love our work, and we are comfortable writing about people who do things for the love of the work. After that, we're quite squeamish about considering or covering love. Sex, sure. Schmaltz, on schmaltzy occasions like Valentine's Day or Mother's Day. Obsession, absolutely, especially if it ends in murder or kidnapping (preferably both). Genuine expressions of love are suspect, because irony doesn't accept genuineness and because we are infused with the framework of psychology-cum-economics, which holds that all human emotions are but expressions of self-interest (at best) and troubled psyches (most likely).

People—We journalists love the people and are offended when the people are hurt or are themselves offended. We love telling people stories because we know people love people stories. We serve the people and get special privileges and status because of it. We cite the people as justification for getting what we want or need. We spend most of our time with professionals, a small subset of the people, and consider most efforts (mostly urged upon us by our bosses or our own professional associations) to get to know the people we serve as asinine pandering.

They, them—There is no they, and therefore no them to blame. There are only we, you, and I.

Journalism, Philosophy, and the Editorial Page

Cole was constantly writing to help formulate his thinking.
This is a rumination on his influences and what light they
shed on building a good newspaper editorial page.

M Y JOURNALISM SKILLS have been shaped and enriched by
reporters, editors, designers, photographers, and graphic artists
in every newsroom in which I have worked. My journalism philosophy
has been strongly influenced by five key figures—three living practitioners and two historical luminaries of the 20th century.

Key figure No. 1: Frank Batten (1927-2009), longtime chairman of
Landmark Communications, for whom I worked for 15 years, was a
conservative Virginia gentleman and a daring journalistic entrepreneur.
Frank produced a statement called "The Duty of Landmark Newspapers."
In 11 paragraphs, his statement spells out a journalistic creed of integrity,
excellence, and community commitment. Here is what it says about editorials: "Our editorials should exhibit vigor and courage, always respectful of contrary opinion, never tailored to the whims of the editor or
publisher."

When I was editor of the *Virginian-Pilot*, we cited "The Duty of
Landmark Newspapers" in newsroom deliberations—especially whenever we were struggling to work out a new idea or practice. This is the
heart of the declaration:

> Warts and problems are at the core of news but they are not all
> of the news. Even against the tide of modern life, people and
> institutions make progress. We should be generous in coverage

of achievement; our pages should reflect the grit, devotion, and durability of the human spirit. Let us nourish hope. . . .

A great newspaper is distinguished by the balance, fairness, and authority of its reporting and editing. Such a newspaper searches as hard for strengths and accomplishments as for weakness and failure. Rather than demoralize its community, the great newspaper will by honest and intelligent journalism inspire people to do better.

Key figure No. 2: Davis "Buzz" Merritt, then editor of the *Wichita Eagle*, defined a successful community as one whose members know what is happening and take responsibility for it. Helping people know what is happening—the good and the bad—is the essence of Frank Batten's message. Buzz Merritt adds to the ideas of nourishing hope and inspiring betterment the notion of helping people take responsibility for what occurs in their communities. That broadens the work of journalism from informing and inspiring to enabling—helping citizens acquire whatever conceptual tools and processes they need to exercise ownership of their communities.

Key figure No. 3: Gil Thelen, then editor of the *State* in Columbia, South Carolina [now James A. Clendinen Professor in Editorial and Critical Writing at the University of South Florida], has given me two key illuminating insights. During the work of the Journalism Values Institute of the American Society of Newspaper Editors (ASNE), Gil talked about the role of a newspaper as the "candid friend" of a community. During the work of the ASNE Change Committee, he talked about journalists acting less as detached observers and more as "committed observers." These conceits are powerful. They are at once concise statements of methodology and of moral judgment. A candid friend cares about you and will not diminish or demean you—but will share constructive criticism and convey uncomfortable truths that you are better off knowing than not knowing, or ignoring, or denying. A committed observer, as observer, fulfills the essential function of bearing witness. Because he or she is committed, this witness persists in monitoring what is happening in the community as long as it is happening and does not flit from one topic to the next, hungry for novelty and immediate gratification or sensation. Gil also introduced me to this insight from C. P. Scott, the celebrated editor of the Manchester *Guardian* from 1872 to 1929: "The function of a good newspaper and therefore a good journalist is to see life steady and see it whole." This resonates with Frank Batten's injunction that a newspaper must cover progress as well as problems, strengths and accomplishments as well as weaknesses and failures.

Key figure No. 4: Joseph Pulitzer, [1847-1911] C. P. Scott's trans-Atlantic contemporary, is best remembered for his role in the yellow-journalism wars with William Randolph Hearst on the low end and for underwriting the Pulitzer Prize on the high end. His contributions to journalism practice and philosophy are more sweeping. His crusades were effective in both building circulation and reforming society because they were based on "broad intelligence underlying accurate informa-tion" and executed with "the skill of the practical psychologist, the stump speaker who knew his audience," biographer W. A. Swanberg concluded. "Pulitzer was the most effective of crusaders because no other editor could match him either in background knowledge or the critical facil-ity." He partnered with his readers, most famously in raising money for building the base of the Statue of Liberty, but more routinely in soliciting their ideas about educational reform and other community issues in St. Louis. His *"Post-Dispatch* Platform," which still runs every day on the edi-torial page, is a statement of progressive, nonpartisan populism. It calls upon his journalistic heirs to "always fight for progress and reform" and to "never be satisfied with merely printing news." His *North American Review* essay calling for the creation of a school of journalism ends with a statement now on the walls of the *Post-Dispatch*, Columbia University, and the National Press Club:

Our Republic and its press will rise or fall together. An able, disinterested, public-spirited press, with trained intelligence to know the right and courage to do it, can preserve that public virtue without which popular government is a sham and a mockery. A cynical, mercenary, demagogic press will produce in time a people as base as itself. The power to mould the future of the Republic will be in the hands of the journalists of future generations.

Based on my experience in the field and my tutoring from Frank Batten, Buzz Merritt, Gil Thelen, and Joseph Pulitzer, this is my core journalism philosophy:

- Journalists depend on citizens in order to do our work. Citizens are essential partners in helping journalists fully grasp what's happening in communities. Citizens are experts in their own lives and aspirations and know aspects of community life in great detail. To earn their respect and aid, journalists must be committed, candid, and caring. When journalists and citizens collaborate, both can flourish.

- Citizens depend on journalists to do their work understanding what's happening in their communities and taking responsibility for it. Journalistic judgment achieves its real value only when it contributes to public judgment. "Merely printing news" is not sufficient. An informed public is not sufficient. An inspired public is not sufficient. For communities to succeed, journalists must help create an informed, inspired, and *engaged* public. The people alone are guarantors of public virtue and self-rule.

- Journalism reaches its full potential when it is humanely intelligent. Humane intelligence requires information, ideas, and imagination, contrary opinions and disinterested criticism, generosity, hope, and courage, and the commitment and capacity to see life steady and whole.

The fifth key figure provides the context in which I can situate my journalism philosophy, although he himself was not a journalist (beyond occasionally writing for journals of opinion, such as the *New Republic* and the *Nation*).

Key figure No. 5: John Dewey, [1859-1952] America's preeminent philosopher of the 20th century, is a central figure in democratic theory. From his work I have figured out that journalism is best understood not as *news and information* but as *democratic inquiry*. Democratic inquiry is the systematic assessment of what is happening in the world that requires the attention and action of citizens.

Here are the building blocks of democratic inquiry that can guide effective editorial and opinion journalism:

- Individuality and interaction. These are cornerstones of Dewey's conception of democracy, which is a way of life and not just a form of government. We realize our individuality in interaction with others. Individuality comes to fruition through equality and freedom. We achieve equality when we achieve equal standing to contribute whatever is distinctive and unique about ourselves to common enterprise. We achieve freedom when we secure the ability to carry out a course of action. This entails more than the "negative freedom" that removes external constraints. It also requires the positive freedom of association with others to develop our capacity. For example, to be free to speak our mind entails more than prohibiting censorship. It also requires someone along the way—family, friends, teachers—to help us learn how to think and speak. To protect individuality, an editorial page must evaluate policies and practices according to how they affect people's equal standing to contribute and their effective freedom to act.

- Ideas, ideals, and imagination. Ideas and ideals help us understand our present circumstances, anticipate future circumstances, and imagine alternatives. Ideas are entry points for investigating current conditions. Ideals are imagined possibilities for improving these conditions. In a democracy, citizens must continually assess how things are working in order to sustain what is good and to secure new goods. Editorial pages are the natural place to explore ideas and ideals—the continuing quest for the good.

- Intelligence in action. Intelligence in action (which Dewey also called social intelligence) occurs when citizens consider the *consequences* of actions and the *conditions* that make it possible to achieve the best consequences. What consequences will follow particular policies and practices? Which conditions will help people and communities realize their full potential? Which will increase participation in democratic life? Such determinations, Dewey scholar Raymond Boisvert writes:

> cannot be accomplished by the isolated thinker seeking direct insight into ideas. They are the product of people working together, gathering information, projecting hypothetically, listening to experts, and debating positions. It is messy, frustrating, too often ill-fated work. But it may be the best we have. It is certainly the method of intelligence most conducive to democratic practice.

Dewey considers social intelligence the best way to produce "warranted assertions"—justifiable statements that in turn justify actions. And it is our only hope for creating and sustaining a truly democratic community. Democratic inquiry involves examining experience and, where appropriate, experimenting with alternative solutions to public problems. It does not begin with what Boisvert terms "a commitment to ideological purity" or "idolatry of fixed antecedent ideological conclusions," because that could privilege ideological correctness over citizens' well-being. To serve democracy and sustain community, then, the work of editorial and opinion pages is not espousing ideology but providing conceptual and communicative space for people to work together, evaluate information and expertise, test hypotheses, debate alternatives—and come to conclusions supported by thoroughly evaluated evidence.

I believe an editorial page must be philosophical, public, deliberative, imaginative, and compelling. It must be philosophical in exploring world views, in contemplating how we know what we know, and in evaluating standards for ethical conduct. It must be public in inviting citizens into the process of making public choices, in helping them develop their full potential, and in helping groups with contrary aims or opinions interact with each other in the pursuit of public judgment. It must be deliberative in requiring warrants for assertions, in respecting wide-ranging points of view, and in modifying its own positions as it learns from others. It must be imaginative in empathizing with others and in envisioning alternative possibilities. It must be compelling in the ways it expresses itself, cheering when the community succeeds, weeping when it suffers, and sweating alongside others when there is work to be done.

FRAMING:
HOW JOURNALISTS—AND
CITIZENS—MAKE FACTS
MAKE SENSE

*This unpublished essay explores framing, a central notion
of public journalism. Framing mattered to Cole precisely
because "traditional" journalists denied they were doing any such
thing. He struggled to make newspapers conscious
of framing as a first step toward building what he considered
the most important frame of all—journalism as a
democratic practice.*

F RAMES ARE AS MUCH a part of journalism as facts. In fact, frames
are what make facts make sense. "There is no way of perceiving and
making sense of social reality except through a frame," Donald A. Schon
and Martin Rein of MIT write, "for the very task of making sense of complex, information-rich situations requires an operation of selectivity and
organization, which is what 'framing' means."

And yet we journalists spend far more attention and discussion on
issues relating to facts—accuracy, interviewing, document searches, data-
base work—than we do on the ways we frame facts in order to make
sense of the world.

What are the key characteristics of framing in journalism?

- <u>Frames set borders and boundaries</u>. In establishing your frame, you are
  deciding which people, places, perceptions, and hard facts to include
  and which to exclude—in a photo, in a story, in a coverage plan.

- Frames emphasize and deemphasize. The way you frame a story puts some people or places or perceptions in the foreground and puts others in the background.

- Frames connect. Frames are sometimes as simple as metaphors, sometimes as complex as analogies. But they serve to make the unfamiliar more familiar—and to make the familiar a bit more exotic, understood in a different perspective.

- Frames orient. A potent frame is a mental model of the way the world works. In the classical world, traveling orators hired to defend at court people they hardly knew relied on these preexisting models (called *topoi*) in the minds of their audiences to quickly sketch the facts and values relevant to a dispute. Think of the political shorthand of "poverty neighborhoods" and "middle-income American comfort" as prefabricated frames—the kind you buy at a craft store instead of a custom frame shop—that writer and reader are presumed to share as standard frames of reference.

- Frames explain—and sometimes preordain. Like a skeleton (the human frame) or the wood beams of a barn, frames also hold things together and make them function in relationship to each other. Larger frames are sometimes referred to as "master narratives," or paradigms.

- Frames refract. The biggest frames—worldviews, belief systems, personal definitions of "The Truth"—can be so pervasive and persuasive that everything you encounter you see through that frame. That makes it hard to consider other frames of reference, other "truths."

- Frames free us. And enslave us. Frames are efficient ways to sort information and create stories. They connect our work to the common understandings of our communities and the larger culture. They make facts meaningful. Frames create "reality." Because they are constructed, they not only can refract but can distort our view of reality or blind us to other views.

The notion of frames flickers in journalism's jargon. We call a time frame of reference a "news peg." We call a simple frame that distinguishes one account of a news event from another an "angle." (But if someone with an interest in the story suggests an angle, we call that angle "spin.") When we discuss narrative writing, we're comfortable with "point of view" and "story lines," which are varying ways to frame the same issue or story.

Even our concept of "story" embodies various frames—the summary frame (conveying the essence of a news event), the narrative frame (telling a story about it), and the production frame (shaping the report as a commodity of expression). Hence the word *story* has three different meanings in these three questions editors often ask reporters: What's the story? How will you tell the story? When can I get the story?

Big thinkers about reality and journalism use big frames. Walt Whitman celebrated newspapers as "mirrors of reality." John Hersey talked about journalism's permissible distortion—we can subtract from reality, but not add to it. William Bradford Huie described himself as being in "the truth business." Ben Bradlee popularized the idea of journalism as "the first rough draft of history." Gene Roberts exhorted his staff to "zig where others zag" as an antidote to the pack-journalism frame. Bill Kovach has pronounced accountability as journalism's raison d'être, without which it could not justify its constitutional protection.

Even the names of our newspapers suggest frames. Newspapers that frame themselves as guardians (*Sentinel, Monitor*), as leaders (*Leader, Statesman, Tribune* and, a courtly adjunct, the *Herald*), as specific identities presumably shared with readers (*American, Tennessean, Democrat, Farmer*), and as means of transmitting or recording information (*Courier, Ledger, Review, Register, Gazette, Journal,* and *Chronicle*). The newspapers I've worked for have compound names that fit the same categories: *Observer* (guardianship); *Pilot, Star* (leadership); *Virginian, Tar Heel* (identities); and *Record, Ledger, Post,* and *Dispatch* (recording/transmitting).

Look at the front page of the St. Petersburg *Times* for Monday, August 21, 2000. Every story had at least one frame—otherwise, it wouldn't make sense—and some stories had more than one.

A story about Tropical Storm Debbie used the threat-to-Floridians frame. A story about a tentative labor agreement between Verizon Communications and its unions used a combined economic/human-impact frame ("a two-week strike affecting 25 million phone users"). A stand-alone photo of Tiger Woods celebrating his PGA Championship overtime win echoes Woods' frame: "This is probably one of the greatest duels I've ever had in my life." An Associated Press report on internal Ford Motor Company documents urging underinflation of Firestone tires on Ford Explorers uses an economic frame (implying that the company urged the underinflation as a cheaper way to reduce the risk of rollovers). And it suggests a powerlessness frame: we are all the potential victims of sneaky corporations.

The grand winner in terms of number of frames was a report on wealthy professionals fleeing Colombia because of drug violence there. This story used the drug war frame, a desertion frame ("Colombians by the thousands are bailing out of their country"), an immigrant/refugee frame, a crisis frame, and an international politics frame ("President Clinton is due to visit Colombia this month in a show of personal support for President Andres Pastranas"). All before the jump.

Having a frame of some sort is inevitable, but it may not be conscious. Each of these frames was chosen to include and exclude some information, to bring to the foreground and push into the background certain information, to connect, to orient, to explain, to refract.

Okay, every story has a frame, just like every person has a belly button. So?

Frames do more than give life to stories in utero, then retreat to collecting lint. They are the determinants of a story's meaning. And frames—master narratives in particular, but resilient metaphors as well—recur over and over again in story after story.

"Everyone, from the greatest genius to the most ordinary clerk, has to adopt mental frameworks that simplify and structure the information encountered in the world," according to J. Edward Russo and Paul J. H. Shoemaker.

> But beware: any frame leaves us with only a partial view of the problem. Often people simplify in ways that actually force them to choose the wrong alternatives. . . . The key to sound decision making is: know your own frames. You need to know how you have simplified your problems. Otherwise, you'll never recognize when you need to reframe and you may lack the self-knowledge necessary to do any reframing well.

Know your own frames. Know how you have simplified the world. Recognize when you need to reframe. Reframe well.

We need to remember that frames also frame our decisions. That's why we need explicit frames, not tacit frames. Are we aware of our frames? Are we letting one frame preempt all others, or are we offering a panorama of frames? Which frame is "truest"? Which is biased? Are we recognizing—or appropriately creating—new frames so culture can grow and political conversation can be richer?

A frame is one way of seeing and portraying a situation. Used exclusively, or applied indiscriminately, it can become a distortion. Know anyone who fits this description from Russo and Shoemaker's *Decision Traps: The Ten Barriers to Brilliant Decision-Making and How to Overcome Them* ? "Poor decision makers (or decision makers who are competent only in narrow fields) may automatically use one or two metaphors to frame almost everything. For example, they may frame everything as a football game, a war, or a family."

One of the most useful studies of framing and journalism comes from W. Russell Neuman, Marion R. Just, and Ann N. Crigler, in their book *Common Knowledge: News and the Construction of Political Meaning.* They interviewed 48 citizens to determine how they framed 5 political issues in the news. Then they assessed how news reports framed the same five issues. They identified five dominant frames used by citizens and journalists alike: the economic frame, the conflict frame, the powerlessness frame, the human-impact frame, and the morality frame. Interestingly, journalists often framed politically powerful figures as pursuing their agendas despite the formidable forces arrayed against them—the powerlessness frame. Journalists used the conflict frame to explain the news 29 percent of the time, while citizens used the conflict frame only 6 percent of the time. Citizens cited the human-impact frame in explaining 36 percent of the news topics; journalists used the human-impact frame half as often.

"It soon becomes clear that in their active interpretation of the political world, audience members alternatively accept, ignore, and reinterpret the dominant frames offered by the media," the authors conclude.

What are the implications of that? Do we widen the gulf between us and our users because we use disparate frames for the same topics? Do we escape allegations of distorting reality if no one relies on our frames anyway?

Should we revisit our master-narrative frames? Consider three examples.

- Campaigns: the winner/loser frame. Jay Rosen of New York University says, "a narrative frame is something set prior to the story, in part because it tells journalists where a good story is to be found." The master narrative for campaign coverage "fleshes out winning as a grand theme. . . . Even issues are easily treated as steps to victory or defeat, because this sort of content is what the frame most comfortably holds. . . . As candidates compete for attention, react to front-page explosions, and try to project through news accounts the image of a winner, they live in the press-created world of winners and losers, attackers and defenders, savvy players and sad sacks. All else that might go under 'politics' is often forced to fit into these standard themes."

- The body politic: the cancer/plague frame. Author Susan Sontag studied the use of illness as a framing metaphor. While AIDS has been described in terms of a plague, with implications of divine retribution, cancer has been cited as the frame for Stalinism and Maoism (by competing communist ideologies), for Watergate and the presidency and, most notably perhaps, for "the Jewish problem" as defined by Hitler. "To describe a phenomenon as cancer is an incitement to violence," Sontag writes. "The use of cancer in political discourse encourages fatalism and justifies 'severe' measures—as well as strongly reinforcing the widespread notion that the disease is necessarily fatal. While disease metaphors are never innocent, it could be argued that the cancer metaphor is a worst case: implicitly genocidal."

- Bloodshed: the Truth frame. Julie A. Mertus went to Kosovo to discover that frames trump facts in group conflict. "Facts are rarely the driving force (behind) human behavior. In terms of their bearing on ordinary human lives, experience and myth are far more persuasive and influential than factual truth. . . . For the most powerful diplomats, the facts could be crucial for determining and assessing blame and for taking action. The people of the region, however, pattern their behavior around what *they* believe to be true, based not on what some outside 'expert' writes but on their own personal experiences and on the myths perpetrated by the local media and other popular storytellers. So for those who are interested in understanding and predicting behavior, what matters is not what is *factually* true but what people believe to be 'Truth.'"

Different frames might produce better journalism—and public discourse. Rosen's assessment of campaign coverage could extend to all three cases: "On the whole, political journalism can be congratulated for connecting us well to the inside story of the campaign, which actually is about winning. The press does less well in connecting the country to its candidates, linking politics to governing, and getting answers to our deeper questions. History has sometimes been called the search for a usable past. Journalism at its best can be a search for a usable present. But its master narratives would have to evolve and improve to do so— and some might need rebuilding or replacement."

The winner/loser, or horse race, frame can generate interest in a political contest, but it also limits the way we conceive of politics. The cancer frame makes cancer seem inevitably fatal—and a disease comparable to the worst of humanity. The "Truth" frame—and particularly, the victimhood frame—can justify all sorts of political violence and bloodshed.

All too often, we select our frames with more reflex than reflection. That can get us into trouble, just as choosing facts poorly can. Think about your frames. Test them. Try out different frames. See what it does for your journalism—and for the citizens who count on your work.

Citations:

Mertus, Julie A. *Kosovo: How Myths and Truths Started a War.* Berkeley, CA: University of California Press, 1999.

Neuman, W. Russell, Marion R. Just, and Ann N. Crigler. *Common Knowledge: News and the Construction of Political Meaning.* Chicago: University of Chicago Press, 1992. See particularly Chapter 4, "Making Sense of the News."

Rosen, Jay. "The Master of Its Own Domain." IntellectualCapital.com. May 11, 2000.

Russo, J. Edward, and Paul J. H. Shoemaker. *Decision Traps: The Ten Barriers to Brilliant Decision-Making and How to Overcome Them.* New York: Simon & Schuster, 1989.

Schon, Donald A., and Martin Rein. *Frame Reflection: Toward the Resolution of Intractable Policy Controversies.* New York: BasicBooks, 1994.

Sontag, Susan. *Illness as Metaphor and AIDS and Its Metaphors.* New York: Anchor Books/Doubleday, 1990.

FROM IMPERILED
TO IMPERATIVE

HOW JOURNALISM MIGHT
MOVE FROM NECESSARY-BUT-
NOT-SUFFICIENT TO
NECESSARY-*AND*-SUFFICIENT

IMAGINE THAT ALL THE BEST that we journalists hope for our craft, our profession, our industry actually exists. That all journalism meets the highest standards of excellence. That all journalism is well crafted. That all journalism is done by competent journalists. That all journalism fulfills journalistic values, with no messy interference from commercial interests of publishers, advertisers, or anyone else with commercial goals. That all journalism commits itself to upholding democracy, and all citizens are reached by a good journalistic print, broadcast, cable, satellite, or online product.

Journalism could still fail—could still be rejected by those it is intended to serve, could still not fulfill a public, socially useful function, could still founder as a business enterprise. That may not be likely—what we journalists think of as high-quality, healthy journalism might have a long life span. But it might not.

In thinking about all the good efforts under way to strengthen journalism, we need to think about a simple proposition from logic: is a condition necessary and sufficient for another condition to exist? Or is it necessary but not sufficient? Oxygen is necessary for multiple life forms on Earth, but it's not sufficient. Any particular reform might be necessary if we aim to strengthen journalism, but is it sufficient? If not, how can we weave together the right fabric to make sure sufficient conditions exist for journalism to prosper? Let's consider journalism through the respective lenses of purpose, craft, and usefulness.

Purpose

Here are seven theses that suggest how all our best efforts to make journalism better may not be sufficient. The first is tied directly to the idea of necessary but not sufficient; the rest elaborate on that theme.

- Work to improve journalism must be more than necessary. It also must strive to be sufficient—in itself or aligned with other work. If all journalism meets internal standards of excellence, but doesn't connect with its users, it can still fail.

- Craft cannot be understood fully or practiced superbly without constant intercourse with purpose and use. If all journalism is well crafted but misconceives its purpose or use, it can still fail.

- Competence is a bar to journalism's salvation. The competent seek to protect their competency, not alter it. If all journalism is done by competent journalists, who feel no vulnerability, it can still fail. (More on the definition of *vulnerability* below.)

- Journalism's primary purpose is not providing information (or entertainment), but sustaining conversations and a commons—where citizens can express a civic identity, make sense of community concerns, and work to reach public judgment. If all journalism consists of sound information, but users can't act, it can still fail.

- Journalism is inherently collaborative. Its value is created by journalists and the people they serve. If journalism reaches every citizen, but doesn't engage citizens, it can still fail.

- A clash in values between newsrooms and boardrooms is neither inevitable nor fatal. The lethal gap is between journalists and citizens, who define useful journalism differently. If all journalism fulfills journalism's highest values, it can still fail.

- Journalists can no longer claim that their work effectively "serves the public" or "upholds democracy" without explaining as concretely as possible their model of democracy. If all journalism commits itself to democracy poorly understood, it can still fail.

In addition to exploring broadly "necessary but not sufficient," these theses also explore the notion that we journalists have a professional point of view about our work, while ordinary citizens tend to have a relational view. That's not to say you and I don't know lots of non-journalists who think of journalism the same way we do. They are probably professionals themselves, or have become professionalized in their viewpoint over time because we have trained them to our viewpoint. Here are some differences that other people may have with professional people in thinking about what makes work, like journalism, excellent and serviceable.

In a professional context, values and standards of excellence are proprietary, set by professionals and relatively fixed. In a relational context, values and standards are shared between the maker and the user and reflect the immediate circumstances confronting them. In a professional context, craft refers to product attributes. In a relational context, craft refers to product benefits—to how useful the product is. In a professional context, competence is a state of completeness, when someone masters all the requisite skills. The competent like their competency and would rather defend it than open themselves up to a critique that suggests they need to supplement their skills or change some of their practices. In a relational context, competence must be tempered by openness, or by being vulnerable to the ideas and experiences of others. In this context, *vulnerability* means "being open to the point of risking something of yourself."

In a professional context, information is conceived as complete and a finished product, an output that people consume, and reaching every citizen is essentially thought of as distribution—or, in media parlance, penetration, reach, or share. In a relational context, information is an ingredient, which citizens treat as a semi-raw, semi-finished input alongside input from friends, neighbors, coworkers, and their own direct knowledge or experience. And distribution matters only if it truly engages people, gets them to actively grapple with the information.

And in a professional context, democracy is treated ritualistically, without a lot of reflection. Journalism serves democracy. End of discussion. In a relational context, democracy is a dynamic concept, realized only by doing something with it. If we assume a model of democracy built around voting, then we produce journalism that serves voting. If we conceive of democracy as active participation of citizens in daily governance, then we produce journalism that serves that participation.

Craft

Here is a wonderful definition of *craft*, from Jedediah Purdy in *For Common Things: Irony, Trust and Commitment in America Today* (New York: Alfred A, Knopf, 1999):

> A marriage of commitment and knowledge produces dignified work. I think of this achievement through the idea of the craftsman, perhaps because I have known craftsmen well and admired their work, perhaps because the solidity of their labor ties ideas to sound and reliable things. His enduring quality of dignity arises from the fact that his work is luminous to him, in its process and its purpose. He understands the application of every tool he uses; many of them he may be able to make or repair himself. He can judge the quality of his materials because he understands what they must contribute to his product and just how that contribution will be made. Because he understands the use of his product as well, he knows just what it is to make it well or badly.

What Purdy describes is the essence of pragmatic liberalism—the movement in society between ideas and "things," or practice. Martin Luther King Jr. was an effective advocate of civil rights because he tied our ideas of liberty, equality, and justice to our practices of segregation and showed them to be unworthy of our ideas. In the same way, scholars move between ideas, expressed as theory, and practices, hoping to use theory to enrich practice and an understanding of practice to enrich theory.

For journalists and journalism educators, this is a reminder that we cannot focus on craft merely as the process or the product—but the relationship of process and product to the purpose of our craft, which informs its process and its product, and the use and usefulness of our journalism, which defines its quality or value and therefore also should inform its process and product.

Usefulness

Since the Enlightenment, journalism has been seen as a solution to the problem of information scarcity—those in power controlled information in order to maintain their power. Journalism has balanced matters, distributing information broadly so readers can hold those with power accountable. But 300 years later, while there are still efforts to suppress information, we face another problem—information overload. Some analysts have seen that journalism as "news" or "information" is an insufficient notion.

In 1912, Joseph Pulitzer urged his heirs and followers: "Never be satisfied with merely printing news." Henry Luce, the founder and publisher of *Time* magazine, made the point more elaborately in a talk to the Women's Club of Stamford, Connecticut, in 1939:

> If people of all classes are far better informed than they used to be, then why is it that we seem to be making just as much

of a mess of our world as ever our ancestors made in the days of their unenlightenment? . . . I will say only this—that just as the answer to the failure and befuddlements of democracy is more democracy, not less, so perhaps the answer to the unfruitfulness of journalism is more journalism, not less. And by more journalism I do not mean more of the same, but rather that journalism must enlarge its field, it must probe deeper, it must and will find a way to deal with those matters which lie most deeply in the nature and will and conscience of men and will make of them great matters, not private whisperings but great public arguments. There are more things in heaven and earth, O Journalist, than are included in your philosophy—or your craftsmanship.

Neil Postman, the cultural critic, makes much the same point in 1999:

If there are people starving in the world—and there are—it is not caused by insufficient information. If crime is rampant in the streets, it is not caused by insufficient information. If children are abused and wives are battered, that has nothing to do with insufficient information. If our schools are not working and democratic principles are losing their force, that too has nothing to do with insufficient information. If we are plagued by such problems, it is because something else is missing. That is to say, several things are missing. And one of them is some way to put information in its place, to give it a useful epistemological frame.

In the 18th century, the newspaper provided such a frame, and given the present information flood, it may be the only medium capable of doing something like that for our use in the century ahead.

Getting to necessary *and* sufficient

Let's engage in a little imaginative thinking. Here are three ways to imagine improving journalism:

Process	Information	Deliberation	Adaptation
Cognitive Method	Find out who knows; extract knowledge; and share it in credible forms	Discover what we know together and work through differences	Attend to stress; interrogate the possibilities; and create ways to live, work, thrive
Goal	Fix accountability	Make choices	Restore equilibrium

In the first column, which I consider the "pragmatic model," journalism is mostly about information used to hold powerful people and institutions accountable. Its main work is to find out who knows what, get that knowledge out into the open, and distribute it broadly through credible means. Tom Rosenstiel and Bill Kovach of the Committee for Concerned Journalists see that this approach to journalism has become battered in recent years, with less-credible news-gathering practices and a fixation on entertainment values undermining journalism's believability and value. So they argue for restoring journalistic practice to higher ideals of information gathering and dissemination. I agree, and I would add that journalism can be improved by exploring and adopting other modes of inquiry, such as field ethnography from anthropology and a host of social-science tools that J. T. Johnson of San Francisco State University argues can contribute to a discipline of "analytic journalism."

In the second column, which I consider the "deliberative model," journalism adds to information the idea of deliberation in order to help people make choices, particularly choices about community issues. Journalism's work expands to include helping citizens learn from each other, create new knowledge through conversation, and support the tough work of citizens (not journalists) making tough choices. Jay Rosen of the late Project on Public Life and the Press, and Ed Fouhy and Jan Schaffer of the Pew Center for Civic Journalism, along with journalists who have been given the name "public journalists" or "civic journalists," believe that journalism can be about information but can support community deliberation more effectively by using a richer conception of democratic practice to shape how information is gathered and disseminated.

In the third column, which I consider the "adaptive model," journalism is about information, deliberation, and adaptation—changing behavior or function in response to social, economic, and political disruptions in order to restore a sense of balance, or equilibrium, within a community. That requires getting a community or organization to pay attention to what really matters, resolving conflicts over what might be done and picking effective decision-making processes in order to select new ways of operating. The idea of transformation and disruption are thoroughly discussed by management guru Peter F. Drucker and historian Francis Fukuyama. The concept of organizational adaptation is explored wonderfully by Ronald Heifetz of Harvard's Kennedy School of Government. But few journalists have begun to study or experiment with these notions.

I see these models as building on each other, almost as nesting boxes. All three require an effective conception of information gathering and dissemination, and the adaptive model builds on the deliberative model by adding the notion of paying attention to the world as being as important as deliberating about the world. It speaks more to what Harry Boyte and others refer to as "public work." Each requires successively greater complexity in process—it's harder to adapt than to deliberate, and harder to deliberate than to gather information. Each pays out a greater return— accountability is important, but making hard choices for the community is even more important, and getting to a state of healthy equilibrium for a community or society is most important.

JOURNALISM AND THE PUBLIC: THREE STEPS, THREE LEAPS OF FAITH

Two of Cole's essays analyzed journalism's flaws
and proposed new ways for journalists to view their work
in relationship to public judgment and public action.
The first is broader, more theoretical in outlook, the second
more specific, addressing a particular news story in
New York City. A third piece notes the boldly imaginative
steps the New York Times took toward public journalism,
even if it would have resisted that term. These
complementary works are presented together here.

THOMAS FRANK, founding editor of the *Baffler*, a magazine of cultural criticism, calls the 1990s "a time of humiliation and cataclysmic decline for journalists." His sweeping summation is at once sobering and sly:

> The news legitimacy crisis could be described in any number of statistical or metaphorical ways, depending on the reporter's requirements: circulation was declining; Generation X was scoffing; other media were encroaching on the turf of network and newspaper; and journalists themselves were blundering wherever one looked, getting it wrong, falling for hoaxes, inventing hoaxes themselves. Then there was that terrifying statistical fact of nature, that mounting tidal wave of public

disgust with the press reflected by poll after poll, by the popularity contests that journalists seemed always to lose. . . . Their social position no longer secure, their power to shape public discourse no longer irresistible, and their traditional prerogatives now the right of any drudge who spoke html or knew how to run a photocopier, journalists were in danger of being demoted altogether, of embarking on that long slide from profession back to mere job. If the Internet was threatening to put the daily newspaper out of business, most of us couldn't wait.

Critics attribute these fundamental flaws to a wide variety of paradoxical explanations. Journalists are undereducated generalists, too ignorant to cover complexity, *and* they are overeducated elites, too out of touch with ordinary people to know what matters. Journalists pander to the masses with sensationalism, and they pander to political elites with "insider baseball" stories glorifying their savvy. Journalists are horribly biased by 1) personal liberalism, 2) corporate owners' conservatism, and 3) the implausibility of anyone seeing the world objectively. Journalists love change because it makes news, and they love the status quo because they like their standing in it. Journalists are anti-social loners and members of a peer-driven pack. Journalists suffer from tunnel vision because they pursue only one thing: Truth. Audiences. Profit. Prestige.

Rethinking notions of knowledge and inquiry

What's causing journalism's troubles? Within journalism, the predominant explanation is that money is the root of all journalistic evil. A wide swath of journalistic heavy hitters argues that a new corporate focus on profits is stripping journalism of resources needed to maintain professional standards. Profit goals impose genuine constraints, and the concentration of media ownership bears careful study. But news companies have always been for-profit commercial enterprises, even during the golden heyday (whenever that was). In fact, only after newspapers became financially successful could they shake free of political patronage and undertake independent reporting.

One core issue does arise from journalism's status as an information business: the way it slices and dices time. C. P. Scott (1846-1932), the editor of the Manchester *Guardian* in England for 57 years, set out an admirable, and much-quoted, standard when he declared, "The function of a good newspaper, and therefore a good journalist, is to see life steady and see it whole." Unfortunately, journalism does not see life steady and whole. It chops up reality into discrete units marked off by weeks, days, hours, and even minutes—whatever the news cycle is for a given news medium. "There can be news without its being daily, but if it were not daily, a news *industry* could never develop," writes historian C. John Sommerville of the University of Florida. "The industry's capital assets would lie idle waiting for news of significance to print. . . . Early editors learned very quickly how to make knowledge *disposable* to insure a steady market."

Journalism exists in the perpetual present, which downgrades the past and cannot anticipate the future. When all time is compressed into the present, immediacy and novelty become paramount—It just happened! It's just about to happen! It's never happened before! Context adds weight to a story when there is room for it or is jettisoned when there isn't. News "decontextualizes everything it reports," Sommerville notes.

> Essentially, daily publication cuts things out of a larger reality in order to dispose of them and clear the decks for tomorrow's edition. There can be little historical or philosophical scale in such reports, because every day's events must be presented as deserving of equal attention. Each day's edition costs the same, after all. You wouldn't buy it tomorrow, because tomorrow's news will supersede today's. Much of the population shares a sort of addiction to this process, which is what news industry profits depend on.

Sommerville argues that fixating on the present has had a profound effect on culture and consciousness. Making news periodical—and thus perishable—means: 1) pushing change, to have more to report; 2) giving the news a forward spin, to orient readers to the next edition; 3) breaking down events into units of fact that seem complete and into narratives that have closure, even if the events themselves are not complete or closed; 4) relating everything to politics as the modern domain for addressing all misfortunes; 5) highlighting conflicts, "which will insure further reports"; 6) adopting an anonymous, institutional voice, to increase the authority of the news organ; 7) focusing on social norms rather than social values, because norms change more rapidly; 8) treating each day as equal "whether the world turned a corner or not"; 9) favoring statistics for their brevity, and 10) keeping news reports simple, short, entertaining, and emotional to encourage their routine consumption.

In summarizing books of literature, history, theology, and philosophy, journalism makes the rest of culture "all a matter of fashion." Periodical journalism treats all ideas as time bound, "so that they need not be refuted, but will expire through neglect." The upshot? "What we get is a teeny bit of our world, vastly enlarged to fill our vision," Sommerville concludes. "You need to go elsewhere for wisdom. Wisdom has to do with seeing things in their largest context, whereas news is structured in a way that destroys the larger context."

Science and other observing professions constantly test and rethink their notions of what constitutes legitimate knowledge and inquiry. Scientists present their findings as uncertain, answerable to a larger body of knowledge and subject to revision as more is learned. In stark contrast, by presenting facts as complete, narratives as closed, and journalistic voice as authoritative, journalism has adopted a false posture of certainty. Anthony Smith, a former director of the British Film Institute and president of Magdalen College of Oxford University, says journalism is undergoing an unconscious crisis because it "has not worked its way through the new issues and problems of knowledge."

> There are 10 ways to describe a fire, 20 reasons for an industrial conflict, 30 versions of the reasons why a set of disarmament talks breaks down, countless "causes" of a kidnapping—all the explanations being equally compelling if one adopts a different time frame or asks a different question or looks toward a different range of consequences. That has always been the case, but in the past the available explanations have been narrower. Today we have access to many more of the possible simultaneous reasons for events. The computers are full of data, all equally available, all ascertainably "true." Journalism has not failed in the sense of being unable to grapple with these or being unaware of them, but in failing to talk to readers, listeners, and viewers as if the world were compounded of uncertainties.

Journalists speak "as if the speaker of news could have no doubt . . . in every story there is a fixed point of certainty, as if the reporter were *telling not enquiring*" (emphasis added). Journalism sees itself as a source of information, not as a means of inquiry. Because it atomizes facts and treats each story as a separate entity, journalism also fails to see itself as "a grand text . . . reflecting and feeding the *mores* of a society."

For a brief time after the attacks of September 11, 2001, journalism regained its nobler profile. News reports offered solace and reassurance to a nation in mourning. When journalism serves to notify people about what's going on, and further bears witness to the unfolding of events, it serves people well through its "news and information" emphasis. So the 9/11 coverage and Claude Sitton's coverage of the Civil Rights Movement both embodied this service function of journalism—notifying people about what's happening, and bearing witness to how it is happening.

Why is this service not enough to sustain journalism against the slings and arrows of its current, outrageous fortune? Because most of the time, we need more than notification and witnessing. The problems of democracy are seldom problems of information. They are instead problems of political will and of what Daniel Yankelovich, the public opinion pioneer, calls public judgment. These problems can be resolved only through public action and public inquiry—not simply through reading, watching, or listening to news and information. People must identify threats and opportunities, work through the range of possible responses, make trade-offs among the alternatives, and come to a shared judgment about what will be done.

Journalism's essential work is not simply providing information. It also must sustain inquiry that can lead to action—helping citizens sort out the contested facts, frames, claims, values, and other elements that shape public judgment and that guide the formation of political will. We citizens need help discerning the choices as we try to make sense of the world and figure out what needs to be done about it. This higher level service—interpretation in service of judgment—is the area in which people increasingly no longer trust journalists to help them make good choices.

Traditional practitioners see themselves as trustees or guardians of what citizens need to know. They don't see themselves as collaborators in helping citizens work through information, claims, values, and beliefs. They do not confer much with citizens; that would entail granting citizens status as partners rather than as customers or clients. The closed culture of newsrooms—which holds that only journalists can understand journalism and make useful suggestions about how to improve it—makes it hard for news organizations to learn (beyond accumulating new facts through daily routines).

I believe the root problem confronting journalism is not so much economic as it is professional. We journalists have become captives of our professional standards, rituals, and relationships—especially with other professionals, whom we privilege as news sources and news subjects. We define knowledge as something possessed by the few—experts and highly educated elites, people in positions of power—and therefore define our job as finding out what the few know and selectively repackaging that for the many.

In the last quarter of the 20th century, journalists were embraced by and incorporated into the American Establishment. "At that moment," writes James Carey of Columbia University, the dean of American communication scholars, "the vaunted progressivism of journalism was abandoned; or, better, journalists accepted the role of progressive intellectuals with a mission to participate in the management of society and simultaneously abandoned the populist wing of progressivism with its dictate to 'afflict the powerful and comfort the afflicted.'" Journalists as a class changed teams, abandoning the craft's partnership with ordinary people and joining other elite, professional factions who would manage public affairs. Journalists now focus coverage on the interests, opinions, and actions of the political and social elite. This is done in the name of serving the people—keeping them informed about what people of status and power are up to. But it has the effect of privileging elites to speak and relegating citizens to listening to their "betters." It's time for journalists to change teams again.

Journalists can take three bold leaps to make journalism more public.

- Connect the pieces. See, and show, how events are tied to underlying political, economic, social systems and structures. Connect the aspirations and challenges in people's lives to political discourse—the problem-solving apparatus—of the community. Describe the whole cumulatively, through reports about the parts. Don't break up the whole into disjointed snapshots. Show us panoramas, not kaleidoscopes.

- Work through the problem of public knowledge. Stop pretending that journalism is a form of unshakeable empirical observation. Most public discourse is not about sorting through news and information, or facts, but about making sense of facts and making sense in the inevitable absence of facts. Journalists should experiment with story forms and reporting processes that help citizens understand common problems, compare trade-offs, and test solutions—to make knowledge, not just receive it. Journalists must be explicit about the frames used to organize facts and humble about what they don't know. They can ask ordinary people to suggest other frames and to fill in the gaps.

- Regard and treat people as experts in their own lives and aspirations. We need journalism that regards citizens as members of the civic community, as producers of public knowledge, and as equal partners with other political actors in creating and shaping the public realm. Public knowledge is generated by the many, in conversations that connect across time, place, and identity—and journalism needs to find ways to help sustain these conversations. Professional journalists can notify, even bear witness. But it takes all of us to make meaningful, and actionable, interpretations. Journalists are well positioned to bring us all, and not just elites, back into the conversation.

Citizens matter, and that's why public journalism matters

The audience in the moot-court courtroom of Saint Louis University School of Law listened appreciatively as Gerald Boyd, deputy managing editor of the *New York Times*, spoke about his life and career. A native son, Boyd had worked for 10 years at the *St. Louis Post-Dispatch*, including a stint in the newspaper's Washington bureau, before joining the *Times* and rising through its newsroom ranks.

After his address, an audience member asked Boyd about tensions in New York between the African American community and the police department following the shooting of Amadou Diallo, the unarmed immigrant gunned down by four police officers in a special crime-fighting unit, and other recent police shootings.

"What is your paper, the *New York Times*, going to be doing to defuse the high tension that has mounted in New York City in the black community?" the audience member asked. "Do you have a strategy for getting these two groups together as far as eliminating the fear that's existed, the suspicions?"

The question reflects a view of the press that has been identified in research commissioned by the American Society of Newspaper Editors: People expect the press to help their communities solve problems. Not solve problems for the community, but help the community solve its own problems. Boyd's answer reflects the contrasting view of a majority of journalists, including those in the audience on this occasion.

"Our role as journalists is basically—I mean, it's kind of trite—but it's to print the news," Boyd said. Beyond that, it is up to the editorial page to offer judgment or campaign for change, he said.

In a panel discussion the next day, I pressed Boyd on his answer. He explained that the *Times* had been covering Mayor Rudolph Giuliani and his handling of the police department very aggressively. Voters can weigh the mayor's performance when they go to the polls in November to decide whether he or Hillary Rodham Clinton should be the next senator from New York. Then he said:

> I think the role of the *New York Times* in the situation with the police shootings is to present all the facts as completely and as timely and as forcefully as it can, so that readers—who we have a lot of faith in—or politicians who're charged with formal police (oversight), or internal groups within the police department, or pressure groups who have such a role in society, can determine how to, or when they want to, react.
>
> That means investigating the shooting, the particulars of the shooting, to no end. It means writing everything we can about the police, the policemen involved. It means writing everything about this unit that these policemen work in. It's writing

everything about the person who was shot as much as we can, and so on and so on and so on.

What Boyd presents as doing-our-job-by-the-book inevitability is actually a formal course based on a political theory about how the world works—or works best. The political theory he articulates is a simple chain, from an event to information about that event, and then to action by select political actors. Even as Boyd affirms *Times* editors' faith in readers, he conceives of the readers' public role primarily as voters. They can express their approval or disapproval of the mayor by furthering or retarding his political ambitions. The real work, he signals, belongs to the officials charged with police supervision, the police themselves, and "pressure groups."

This political theory is grounded on that of Walter Lippmann, who dismissed the American public as a "phantom" in the 1920s and argued that modern life is too complex to be left to citizens to manage. Lippmann favored placing public business in the care of public-spirited elites, better informed and more sensible than the craven masses. The role of the journalist, in Lippmann's view, is to keep the masses informed of what their betters are up to, using the "hot glare of publicity" as a constraint against elites becoming too self-serving. If voters feel ill served, well, they can vote the rascals out come November.

There is a competing sense of how politics works, and how it can work better. This theory does not reduce the public to craven masses or disgruntled voters but treats people as citizens who have much to contribute to public life—as experts in their own lives and as authorities on their own aspirations. This theory, propounded by John Dewey in direct response to Lippmann, expands the chain from event-information-action to event-information-deliberation-action.

And that's what the questioner in St. Louis was asking Gerald Boyd: What can the *New York Times* do about "getting these two groups together" to work through the tensions between them?

Every aspect of the *Times*' coverage of police shootings that Boyd describes is vitally necessary. The accumulation of details creates what philosophers call "thick description." As bioethicist Carl Elliott has said: "We want to know about the characters who are involved, their histories, their flaws and virtues, what their consciences are telling them. We want to know them because these details are important morally. If there is anything that practical ethics has taught us, it is that genuine moral experience is rich in detail, and it is often on these rich details that our minds are made up or changed."

But providing detailed information is not sufficient by itself. Information alone rarely makes the appropriate action self-evident. And all too often, elites—including most professionals and most journalists—favor information from those at the top of social and political hierarchies. Some classes of people are actively sought out by journalists to join in a community's conversation, while others are minimized or left out. Their only role is to eavesdrop on what the others are saying.

Daniel Yankelovich, who moved from the study of public opinion to the study of public judgment, writes:

> The theoretical justification for excluding the public from policy formation is based on a narrow hierarchical conception of knowledge that excludes the wisdom of the collectivity— arguably the most indispensable virtue of sound policy. Instead of levels of knowledge within a hierarchy, we ought to visualize a variety of ways of knowing, each designed to meet a different purpose, each with its own ground rules and its own excellences and limitations.

Wisdom is not the outcome of accumulated facts but rather the outcome of working through facts, values, and aspirations to reach public judgment.

And so we come to public journalism. Its guiding principles include:

- Treating citizens as experts in their own lives and aspirations—and therefore legitimate sources of news, information, and context.

- Treating citizens as political actors who can create public knowledge by deliberating together.

- Creating new forms of storytelling and reporting to enrich information.

Given that guidance, how might the *New York Times* have framed its police-shooting coverage to—in the phrase of G. Michael Killenberg and Robert Dardenne—"direct and enhance community discourse"? Their students at the University of South Florida posed these questions in a similar incident in St. Petersburg: "What does the community expect from its police? What values are at stake for the community as a whole when police enforce the law aggressively? How are police selected and trained? What attributes are most valued within a police culture? What attitudes do residents have toward police and vice versa?"

What would the *Times* do in the political arena? It would ask contingent questions, such as if Giuliani wants to win upstate New York, what must he do?

Why couldn't the *Times* ask similar contingent questions of citizens: If New York City is to get past racial tensions over police work, what can be done? What are you willing to do?

Or, as suggested by the questioner in St. Louis, the *Times* could have convened conversations among citizens and police, just as it now convenes one-on-one conversations called interviews. Or it could have covered citizen deliberation as it occurred across the three boroughs, just as the paper might cover the meeting of a government panel.

Such coverage might not have made a difference. Or it might have accelerated public deliberation by spotlighting it and showing how it works. It might have eased tensions as citizens read about other citizens working through issues. At a minimum, it would have reassured average people that their wrestling with these questions mattered and was being taken into account by at least one powerful institution in the city—the newspaper.

The essence of public journalism is that it values citizens. It tries to fit journalistic practice to democratic theory and to democratic practice. Public journalism is imperfect, but so are humanity, democracy, and everything else we journalists cover.

The *New York Times* reimagines journalism

The *New York Times Magazine* took *Times* journalism in a new and inspiring direction Sunday, September 8, 2002, across the threshold of civic imagination and into the realm of public journalism, seeking to open up—rather than close down—public deliberation about the future of the World Trade Center site and all of Lower Manhattan.

"Don't Rebuild. Reimagine," exhorts the headline on a story by *Times* architecture critic Herbert Muschamp. The accompanying large-type lead-in to the story explains the *Times*' public purpose: "Now is the time for New York to express its ambitions through architecture and reclaim its place as a visionary city."

Imagination. Public deliberation. A declared public purpose other than retread references to the public's right to know. This was a declaration of the public's right to imagine and deliberate—and the *Times*' commitment to helping both occur in the name of a public good: restoring New York City to its paramount role among the world's cities, given that a city is "the paramount learning device of civilization."

And so the *Times* convened a team of renowned and up-and-coming architects and engineers, who

> gathered at a series of loud, contentious meetings. They argued over core principles, lobbying one another by phone and FAX. Eventually, they reached something like an agreement—or at least the broad strokes of one. Then each one was assigned a specific site and task and asked to supply a corresponding image.

Over a 14-page spread, the magazine offers the team's architectural sketches and site plans. The designs show how offices, homes, stores, restaurants, community centers, cultural institutions, and memorials can be constructed not only in a respectful restoration of Lower Manhattan's lost square footage but also in an interrelationship to each other that creates "a living memorial to those who died in last year's attack." The designs include fantastical buildings that suggest both structural vulnerability and spiritual resilience—provocative antidotes to what Muschamp describes as New York's "viciously anticosmopolitan program" in its recent architecture. But the most important aspect of the design package is its incompleteness, its gaping holes, its humility in being grand architecture offered up only as a suggestion to keep public deliberation moving along.

"The plan builds on some ideas that are already in circulation and is meant only as an offering to the public conversation," the editors say in introducing the package. "Many features remain hotly contested even among members of the team. . . . The plan that follows is an incitement to the city to think big. It is a celebration of the power of architecture to inspire, to dazzle—and to spur furious debate." Muschamp concurs, saying it is "not a comprehensive plan, but an integrated set of options for the future of New York." The same deadlines that keep most journalism projects from being fully realized also kept the architects from focusing on some critical issues.

Yes, this was a piece in the Sunday magazine. Yes, it was written by a critic. So straitlaced journalistic teetotalers might point to these elements as ingredients for an intoxicating elixir that might excuse, or at least explain, the *Times* slipping free of the journalistic presumption that description trumps imagination, authoritative declaration trumps public deliberation, and impartial witnessing trumps public prophecy.

But the *Times* editors don't exonerate their inventiveness that way. Their main justifications for their journalistic deviance are two: the public purpose—New York shouldn't settle for just "getting back to normal"— and the humility of their offering, despite its lofty parentage. The *Times* refers to the drawings and site plans repeatedly as merely an architectural study and input for public discussion.

The editors also lay out the traditional elements of their approach as an implicit defense. Several of the architects already had met to complain about the official design process, so the *Times*' follow-up did not entrap them in the commission of a *cri de coeur* they would not otherwise have uttered. The official design process was flawed, which the *Times* would be expected to expose just as it would expose a flawed budgetary process or military planning process. The editors acknowledge that the magazine's "urging" helped the architects become "more productive" by "doing what architects rarely do with one another—collaborating." But they do not say what makes a news organization's urging effective—or legitimate. They lack a vocabulary to describe in journalistic terms what they have done, so they borrow terminology from art and culture: "The magazine invited Herbert Muschamp, the *Times*' architecture critic, to curate for our pages an exhibit of their ideas."

Thus the *Times* adds "exhibit" alongside "exposé" and "explanatory journalism" to its menu of journalistic forms. And *Times* journalists can now be political reporters, narrative storytellers, or exhibit curators. Contained within this metaphorical adaptation are great leaps forward in the *Times*' conception of journalism:

- It's okay for a news organization to move beyond describing a situation—in this case, public and professional discomfort with the design process for rebuilding Lower Manhattan—toward imagining what might be done to improve, fix, or otherwise address the situation. The key for a news organization is to frame its imaginings as one offering among many—and to encourage others to offer their ideas and suggestions, too, through the news organization's means of publishing or broadcasting, as the *Times* does on its website.

- It's okay for a news organization to open up public deliberation and to offer experts on tap, not on top—to use expertise to illuminate problems and possible solutions while acknowledging that actual solutions such as the final form of a World Trade Center memorial should "emerge from a vigorous public debate."

- It's okay for a news organization to act on, and declare upfront, a public purpose when it initiates enterprise journalism, whether that enterprise is an exposé, an explanatory series, or an exhibit of provocative ideas. When a news organization pursues an explicit public purpose, it's okay for it to use what the late John Gardner of Common Cause called "convening authority"—the authority to call people together to deal with public issues. That's what the *Times* did not only in explicitly calling together the architects to collaborate but also in implicitly calling together its community of readers to respond to its "incitement to the city to think big."

The Sunday magazine's breakthrough builds on what James Fallows described in *Slate* as the *Times'* tremendous "organic response to genuinely important news" throughout its coverage following the attack on the World Trade Center and the Pentagon. Fallows particularly cited the community solace offered by the *Times'* "Portraits of Grief," profiling victims of the attack.

Fallows found it ironic that Executive Editor Howell Raines, a once rancorous critic of journalism aimed at sustaining communities and encouraging public engagement, could now be hailed as a leading practitioner of what has come to be called "public journalism." "When journalism schools of the future do their studies of what public journalism means," he concluded, "their shining example will be the *New York Times* under Howell Raines."

The *Times'* call to reimagine Lower Manhattan—and the way the *Times* therefore reimagines its own journalism—is more evidence that Fallows may well be right.

DELIBERATIVE DEMOCRACY AS NESTED PUBLIC SPHERES

Because he read so widely, one of Cole's strengths was his ability to connect and integrate the work of many writers. This essay, written for the Kettering Foundation, displays that strength as he discusses Charles Taylor's contribution to the study of public life.

EVEN AS WE PROCLAIM democracy ascendant around the globe, nagging doubts persist about how it can work effectively in increasingly complex—and now global—societies. How can citizens connect to each other despite diverse backgrounds and beliefs? How can they connect to regional, national, and transnational governing bodies? How can they take time from their individual lives to competently oversee their common lives? Given the rise of Big Business, Big Government, and Big Philanthropy, how does citizen action fit into the arenas of state, market, and civil action?

Charles Taylor, professor of philosophy at McGill University in Montreal, Canada, is one of the world's preeminent living philosophers. He has written an essay addressing many of these issues. The essay, "Liberal Politics and the Public Sphere," concludes Taylor's book, *Philosophical Arguments* (Harvard University Press, 1995). Taylor's essay gives us a road map of how deliberative democracy can work. This summary, with extensive quotations from the essay, ends by linking Taylor's insights with those of some other scholars of public life.

Taylor reminds us that a liberal society seeks to maximize freedom and collective self-rule while protecting individual rights and respecting the equality of its members. To this end, the liberal tradition has developed a variety of associations, generally considered nonpolitical, that make up what we call civil society. "No society can be called free in which these voluntary associations are not able to function," Taylor emphasizes, "and the pulse of freedom will beat very slowly where they are not being spontaneously formed."

In the West, civil society has taken two major forms: the public sphere and the market economy. Both are largely (but not completely) extrapolitical—beyond politics. Both are secular: they exist not as an expression of divine will, or nature, or "the great chain of being … or by a law coming down to us since time out of mind," but as a result of the actions of those working in each domain. That lets each domain serve as a check on power and as a bulwark of freedom.

The public sphere is the field of "common action."

> The public sphere is the locus of a discussion potentially engaging everyone … so that the society can come to a common mind about important matters. This common mind is a reflective view, emerging from critical debate, and not just a summation of whatever views happen to be held in the population. So it has a normative status: government ought to listen to it.

Government ought to listen because the outcome of deliberation reflects both rational discussion and the will of the people who worked through the issues. The market economy is not the field of common action, but of multiple interactions, "in which a myriad of small-scale, bilateral common actions generate an overall pattern, behind the backs of the agents, by an invisible hand."

The public sphere and public opinion

"What is a public sphere?" Taylor asks.

> I want to describe it as a common space in which the members of society meet, through a variety of media (print, electronic) and also in face-to-face encounters, to discuss matters of

common interest; and thus to be able to form a common mind about those matters. I say "a common space" because, although the media are multiple, as well as the exchanges taking place in them, they are deemed to be in principle intercommunicating. The discussion we may be having on television right now takes account of what was said in the newspaper this morning, which in turn reports on the radio debate of yesterday, and so on. That's why we usually speak of the public sphere, in the singular.

The public sphere is now so central to modern society's self-justification as free and self-governing that "even where it is in fact suppressed or manipulated, it has to be faked. Modern despotic societies have generally felt compelled to go through the motions"—editorials in party papers urging reflection, mass demonstrations voicing indignation—"as if a genuine process were in train of forming a common mind through exchange, even though the result is carefully controlled from the beginning."

The public sphere's true innovation is its rich conception of public opinion—the process of forming a common mind. This public opinion differs from earlier notions of "general opinion" or "the opinion of mankind," which was considered unreflective, unmediated by discussion and critique, and inculcated passively in each successive generation.

> Public opinion, by contrast, is meant (1) to be the product of reflection, (2) to emerge from discussion, and (3) to reflect an actively produced consensus. . . . We share a common public opinion, if we do, because we have worked it out together. We don't just happen to have identical views; we have elaborated our convictions in a common act of definition.

Two distant strangers could hold a shared opinion because they have been socialized in the same way. But in the case of public opinion:

> Something else is supposed: that the two widely separated people sharing the same view have been linked in a kind of

space of discussion, wherein they have been able to exchange ideas and reach a common end. . . . In the formation of public opinion each of these linked physical or print-mediated encounters is understood by the participants as forming part of a single discussion proceeding toward a common resolution.

The public sphere emerged in the 18th century in part because printing and "print capitalism" created the infrastructure to support it. People could circulate printed materials from a variety of independent sources to feed and reflect a common discussion. Beyond a technological infrastructure, Taylor says, the public sphere requires a cultural infrastructure —a cultural context of "attending to the common object, or purpose, together, as against each person just happening, on his or her own part, to be concerned with the same thing. In this sense, the opinion of mankind offers a merely convergent unity, while public opinion is supposedly generated out of a series of common actions."

The public sphere and power

The public sphere lets people realize their sovereignty by giving them the means to produce a common mind—and common sense. Government is both wise and morally bound to follow public opinion, "to be concentrating and enacting what has already been emerging out of enlightened debate among the people." Jürgen Habermas, the German philosopher, and Michael Warner of Rutgers University have termed this the "principle of supervision," the insistence that:

> The proceedings of governing bodies must be public, open to the scrutiny of the discerning public. In this way legislative deliberation informs public opinion and allows it to be maximally rational, while at the same time exposing itself to its pressure, and thus acknowledging that legislation should ultimately bow to the clear mandates of this opinion. . . . This comes to be seen as an essential feature of free society. . . . As Habermas puts it, power was to be tamed by reason.

In the ancient Greek city-state, citizens might informally discuss governmental action in the marketplace, then convene as a formal body to decide the matter officially. In both informal and formal settings, citizens held power. In contrast, the modern public sphere "is a space of discussion which is self-consciously seen as being outside power. It is supposed to be listened to by those in power, but it is not itself an exercise of power." Being outside power lets the public sphere be "ideally disengaged from partisan spirit."

The public sphere upends

> the old ideal of a social order undivided by conflict and difference. On the contrary, it means that debate breaks out and continues, involving in principle everybody, and this is perfectly legitimate. The old unity will be gone forever. But a new unity is to be substituted. For the ever-continuing controversy is not meant to be an exercise in power, a quasi-civil war carried on by dialectical means. Its potentially divisive and destructive consequences are offset by the fact that it is a debate outside power, a rational debate, striving . . . to define the common good.

As Warner says: "It silently transforms the ideal of a social order free from conflictual debate into an ideal of debate free from social conflict."

"So what the public sphere does," Taylor writes, "is to enable the society to reach a common mind, without the mediation of the political sphere, in a discourse of reason outside power, which nevertheless is normative for power."

Some people argue that the most important task of civil society is to limit potentially all-intrusive state power.

> Let the market economy be as free of state interference as it is possible to make it. Let the public sphere be as clearly demarcated from the political as can be, constituted at the limit exclusively by media that claim total political neutrality. The

camp is deeply imbued with the idea that the extrapolitical is the main bulwark of freedom.

Others argue that a liberal civil society

must also be concerned with self-rule, that is, it must strive to make power and in general whatever shapes the conditions of our lives responsive to collective decisions. . . . From this standpoint, the public sphere plays not only a limiting, whistle-blowing role. It also can serve or disserve, raise or lower, facilitate or hamper the common debate and exchange which is an intrinsic part of conscious, informed collective decision.

The public sphere and citizens

In a democracy, "rules and decisions ought to be determined by the people," Taylor notes.

This means that (1) the mass of the people should have some say in what they are going to be, and not just told what they are; that (2) this say should be genuinely theirs, and not manipulated by propaganda, misinformation, irrational fears; and that (3) it should to some extent reflect their considered opinions and aspirations, as against ill-informed and knee-jerk prejudices.

That can seem utopian. Some political thinkers believe the average voter is too ill informed, and too distracted, to cast an enlightened ballot. Powerful interests can use the media, major parties, propaganda, and money to manipulate public debate.

Citizens can be alienated in a centralized, bureaucratic world. Citizens can be divided into warring classes or groups that feel excluded and ignored. With citizens alienated and divided, political life can become fragmented. In such a state, people mobilize around smaller interests and disavow the search for the general good. Politics shifts to courtroom battles with winner-take-all outcomes, or to interest-group, advocacy politics in which rights are asserted as trump cards and consensus is hard to reach on tough issues that require some parties to make sacrifices. Sound familiar?

"A fading political identity makes it harder to mobilize effectively, and a sense of helplessness breeds alienation," Taylor writes.

> Now we can see how in principle the vicious circle might be turned into a virtuous circle. Successful common action can bring a sense of empowerment, and strengthen identification with the political community. Indeed, the debate on certain kinds of issues, which foregrounds common goals, even with radical disagreements about the means, can help make the sense of political community more vivid, and thus offset the tendency of deep political divisions to paint the adversary as devoted to utterly alien values.

Citing Alexis de Tocqueville's warnings about centralized government, Taylor argues for decentralizing not only government and politics but also our model of the public sphere.

> Just as in politics, local concerns may impinge only with great difficulty on the center; so the national debate may become concentrated in a small number of mass media that are impervious to local input. The sense becomes widespread that the debate on the major television networks, for instance, is shaped by relatively narrow groups or interests, and its animators operate within a charmed circle that can't be penetrated. Other views, other ways of posing the question, other agendas cannot get a hearing.

Taylor argues for localized government and "nested" public spheres. When decisions are made locally, local media can focus on the debate by the people who will be affected by the decision. "The national debate can be changed as well by effective local spheres. The model that seems to work here is one in which smaller public spheres are nested within larger ones, so that what goes on in the smaller ones feeds into the agenda of the national sphere." That "can mediate the input from masses of ordinary citizens, who otherwise feel excluded from everything but the periodic national elections."

Political parties and social movements "can function as nested public spheres to the extent that their internal debate is open to the public. . . . Some of the most effective nested public spheres are in fact political parties and advocacy movements, which operate in the gray zone between the two. In a modern democratic polity, the boundary between political system and public sphere has to be maximally porous." Political parties can build broad coalitions on issues. Social movements can mobilize people not routinely involved in politics. As people and ideas move between politics and social movements, both are enriched and the public sphere acts as "a medium of democratic politics."

John Dryzek, a professor of social and political theory at Australian National University, offers in *Political Theory*, October 2001, two ideas that build on Taylor's notion of nested public spheres. Dryzek says that people are drawn to different discourses about public life, which are often in contest with one another. For example: some people believe criminals are rational actors who calculate the gains of crime against the risk of punishment, while others believe criminals are created by economic and social deprivations and still others believe that criminals are not rational but are sociopathic or psychopathic. Each of these discourses—or frames, or master narratives—leads to different ideas about crime prevention and correction. People who embrace different discourses can learn from others through deliberation, Dryzek says, and public policy that resonates with different discourses within society is usually seen as politically legitimate. This suggests that nested public spheres can be overlapping discourses as well as overlapping associations, each influencing others and the formulation of public policy.

Dryzek also notes that networks frequently arise around different discourses. These networks are not hierarchical or centralized; they simply link people with similar experiences or interests. The links can lead to new understandings and concepts. He cites the environmental justice network, which arose as communities were wrestling with the immediate threats of toxic pollutants in their neighborhood. As people collaborated within the networks, they came to realize that toxic pollutants were more likely to be dumped or stored in neighborhoods with less economic, political, or social power—and thus their interests expanded from dealing with immediate toxic threats to dealing with the longer term injustices that led to the toxic threats arriving in their neighborhoods. These networks are another example of nested public spheres linking people to neighbors, to strangers similarly situated, and to larger political bodies.

Putting nested public spheres to work

Taylor's notion of nested public spheres helps us understand how self-rule can survive, and flourish, in a complex, global world. Individual citizens can gain access to democratic politics by connecting to a local association or forum—or by identifying with and joining a distinct discourse about a public issue. Citizens do not have to be connected to each other in word or deed on every public issue—and in fact cannot be, given the size of most modern democracies and the number of public issues under discussion. Citizens can enter or leave deliberations "as they see fit," in Dryzek's phrase, according to their own interests and desires. "At any given time, the contestation of discourse can be engaged by the many or the few, or indeed by none," Dryzek writes. "Typically, that number will fluctuate widely over time for any given issue area; think, for example, of the upsurges in environmental concern in most developed countries around 1970 and again around 1990."

Michael Schudson of the University of California, San Diego, elaborates on this dynamic through the archetype of the "monitorial citizen," who enters the public sphere on occasion to monitor issues that matter to him or her and relies on other citizens to keep watch on other issues. Journalists Bill Kovach and Tom Rosenstiel offer a similar "Theory of the Interlocking Public," which envisions an involved public of people with a direct stake and understanding of an issue, an interested public affected by an issue at a remove, and an uninterested public, which pays little attention. "In the Interlocking Public, we are all members of all three groups, depending on the issue," they write.

Citizens engaged with associations or discourse can teach and learn from each other, pooling their collective intelligence. They can argue within their association or across discourses without fear of powerful reprisal, because their arguments take place in a sphere outside of power. And the very act of arguing can unite and build social cohesion across differences, without requiring consensus. Citizens' local associations and forums can create effective state and national umbrella organizations to tie them into national deliberations, just as local conversations can shape and be shaped by national discourse. News media that have developed a public or civic orientation can help connect citizens to what Todd Gitlin of New York University calls "public sphericules" and can connect such sphericules—or nested public spheres—to each other.

Nested public spheres are the means that take us from Margaret Mead's admonition—"Never doubt that a small group of thoughtful, committed citizens can change the world; in fact, it's the only thing that ever has"—to our experience with national apparatuses that make policy. Public life stretches across a broad canvas, from six householders around a kitchen table in Tupelo, Mississippi, to nine Supreme Court justices along a bench in Washington, DC.

Participation in small-group deliberation and studies of groups that engage in deliberation and public contestation are more than academic or civic "feel-good" exercises. Such participation and studies are pathways into how democracy operates—and how it can operate more effectively.

REIFYING, DEIFYING, AND DEMONIZING "THE PUBLIC": LET'S CALL THE WHOLE THING OFF

Cole wrote this shortly after 9/11/2001.
Though he referred to it as "a slight provocation,"
this essay is a serious exploration—by a man
who cared about language— of the meaning of a
word easily and often taken for granted.
It was presented to the Committee on Politics,
Philosophy, and Public Policy at the
University of Maryland.

O N SATURDAY, September 15, 2001, four days after terrorists hijacked civilian airliners and crashed into the World Trade Center, the Pentagon, and Pennsylvania, five prominent American journalist-commentators discussed the political and military implications of "America's New War" on the CNN program *The Capital Gang*.

The discussion was wide-ranging, interspersed with video clips of President Bush, Secretary of State Colin Powell, Senator Hillary Rodham Clinton, Prince Bandar Al-Saud of Saudi Arabia, and others. Throughout the discussion, the Capital Gang offered their portrait of one key component of America's response to terrorism: The Public.

The portrait was a familiar caricature.

Kate O'Beirne of the *National Review* said that "the way The Public now views" international cooperation against terrorism is: "You are either with us or against us on this one. . . . And The Polls tell us—and I'm not surprised to see it—that The Public is 100 percent practically in favor of a massive military response to this attack on us."

Mark Shields, the host, concurred. "I mean, revenge is in the air, there's no question about it. I mean, in every measurement of Public Attitudes—and I've never seen it as high. I mean, that sense of vengeance. How long will that survive? I mean, just from your own experience and your own analysis, how long is that—does it have a shelf life of a month, six months, or a year?"

"Well, until last week," Margaret Carlson of *Time* magazine replied, "as a matter of principle This Country was willing to commit no ground troops, it seemed, for any reason. A body bag was unacceptable."

"You know, we're talking about years, we're not talking about months," Al Hunt of the *Wall Street Journal* said. "We're talking about the loss of a lot of American lives in this over the long run. . . . There are going to be retaliations."

O'Beirne jumped back in, addressing first Shields and then Robert Novak of the *Chicago Sun-Times*:

> Mark, I'm not a military planner, so I'm not exactly sure what our military planners spent much of today planning. I do know this, though: I do think that the people who think that The American Public will not stand for casualties really exaggerate The American Public's concern.
>
> Polls showed, Bob, during the Persian Gulf War—people were being told constantly that that war was going to cost us thousands of body bags. It, thank God, didn't. But The American Public still, if they know it is in our interests—and, boy, after Tuesday, defending America from future attacks like this— there is every reason to believe The American Public will have, I think, a realistic view of what the cost could be.

"That isn't the point," Novak responded. "The point is—I think The

American People ought to be willing to suffer, to have their sons and daughters killed for a cause they believe in."

Later, the capital gangsters turned to President Bush's standing with The Public during what Shields called the "first really big crisis of his presidency."

O'Beirne praised the president's visit with rescue workers in Lower Manhattan and his remarks at the memorial service at the National Cathedral in Washington. "So I think he came through," she said, "and The Polls certainly seem to indicate The Public overwhelmingly agrees. I think he came through the week in a really strong position."

"Al Hunt, the president's Polls are stratospheric," Shields said. "The question—docs it— is it a rally to the flag, and the president is the flag at this point? How strong and reassuring was he earlier in the week, did you think?"

"We—of course The Polls reflect the rallying around him. You know, the same thing happened with his dad back in 1991," Hunt replied. Then he shifted to a future-oriented perspective:

> A year from now, if we have done away with Osama bin Laden, we have terrorism on the run, he's kept together a very important international coalition, doesn't matter how he did this week. And on the other hand, if terrorism has us on the run a year from now, it also doesn't matter how he did this week. He's going to be judged by deeds, not words.

The proper-noun capitalization is mine, for emphasis, but the personification is theirs: *The Public*—at times synonymous with *This Country* and *The American People*, manifested in *Public Attitudes* and *The Polls*—is an abstraction made concrete.

The scholarly and professional literature abounds with works arguing that citizens have been elbowed out of democratic politics in the United States. Some works blame cagey political (or economic) elites. Some blame apathetic and self-absorbed citizens. Some cite certain Progressives' pure-minded insistence on professionalizing public life, while others echo the corollary world-weary worldview popularized by Walter Lippmann that citizens are unworthy of self-rule except, during election years, by broadly consenting to—or throwing out—any particular political administration.

I want to add another suspect to the list of those likely to be elbowing citizens out of politics: The Public—as invoked by the Capital Gang and many of us who talk, write, and think about politics, philosophy, and public policy.

The problem of *The Public*

The word *public* has a problematic role in discussing democracy, politics, and even concepts that incorporate the word into their phraseology, such as public life. The first problem occurs in the use of *public* as a modifier, because it means so many different things. Among them: "popular," as in public acclaim; "open to all," as in public park, public domain, and public toilet; "accountable to outsiders," as in certified public accountant, public utility, and maybe even public scrutiny and public relations; "nonprofessional," as in a public member of a professional or regulatory board; even "outdoor," as in public art. Two meanings in particular fit discussions of democracy and politics: "owned by government," as in public schools and public policy, and "not private," as in public interest, public figure, public persona, and public display of affection.

. In my field, the problematic nature of *public* as modifier is evident in the term *public journalism.* Many journalists drop in an assumed meaning of public as adjective and think of public journalism as popular (or, more dismissively, pandering) journalism or as nonprofessional (or, more dismissively, unprofessional) journalism. Even more threatening to some is accountable-to-outsiders journalism. Others wonder what the presumed alternative—private journalism—looks like. I don't propose to rehash the public journalism debate, although I will return to it to illustrate how a more rigorous definition of *public* as modifier might apply to a discipline like mine or yours.

The problem that particularly concerns me is the use of *public* as noun. When we place the article in front, The Public suddenly becomes at once central and marginal. We extol The Public and yet eviscerate it by limiting its range of action. Political actors persuade, mobilize, manipulate, or engage The Public, which makes The Public central to public discourse. But The Public itself can only approve/support/comply/ acquiesce ("be willing to suffer," as Novak said) or disapprove/oppose/ defy/resist—in other words, respond as a target that has been otherwise marginalized.

For The Public to become a visible target, we must embody it. The Public very quickly becomes Public Opinion (or Shields' Public Attitudes), and Public Opinion very quickly becomes The Polls. Or The Public becomes Whoever Shows Up at a demonstration or public hearing or "external lobbying," such as letter-writing campaigns. For most political actors, The Public is Them, although for some civically inspired actors, The Public is a solipsistic version of Us.

The upshot is that we muddle our notions of political authority and agency. We confound legitimacy with popularity. And we devalue real political actors: citizens, their designated agents, and their delegated-to associations and institutions.

What we get from this muddle is the perpetual campaign, in which every public policy option is measured in terms of immediate public support. Do the proponents of the policy have it? Can they get it? Can they keep it? These questions have framed national dialogue about presidential impeachment, the Chinese downing of an American surveillance plane and, now, how the US government responds to terrorism.

Four days after thousands of people died in this heinous attack, well before their bodies were recovered from the still-smoking debris, pollsters and pundits were tracking—*and discussing as if it mattered*—the president's ratings in public opinion surveys.

The Capital Gang portrays The Public as a central figure in what might be done in answering terrorism. But The Public's role is limited to offering or withholding approval—for the president's style of command and compassion, for the eventual outcome of his actions in suppressing terrorism, for stacking their sons and daughters in body bags. The Public has no acknowledged role in working through a range of options that might involve players other than the president and those he can direct or cajole. And The Public is fickle—intolerant of body bags last week, hot for vengeance today; rallying to the president as our patriotic patriarch for the moment, but apt to condemn him a year hence if he doesn't deliver Osama bin Laden's head on a platter.

The Public is divorced from any role in deciding what *ought* to be done—by means of a myriad of military, diplomatic, economic, and domestic responses. The Public is divorced from any responsibility for what *will* be done—through military suppression and casualties. The only political actor who counts is the president—and such subordinate political actors, domestic and foreign, as he chooses to hold accountable. Citizens are elbowed out of any politics other than the politics of approval/opprobrium.

Invoking the nominal public—*The Public* as noun, as existing in name only, as a trifle, as an abstraction with no independent existence beyond its invocation—has consequences beyond mere semantic or philosophical rumination. And so I have been wondering for some time: What if those of us who speak, write, and think about politics, philosophy, and public policy abandoned *The Public?* What if we self-consciously chose other nouns—*citizens, associations, institutions*—to designate political actors acting in concert? What if we preferred other phrases—*the public realm, the public sphere*—to designate where the dynamics of public relationships unfold? What if we restricted use of *public* to an adjective— and defined precisely the attributes that adjective signifies? Might there be a correlating real-world shift in who is understood to have political agency and authority? Might citizens be elbowed back into democratic politics?

In assailing the nominal public, I deviate from my exemplars. John Dewey titled his 1927 treatise *The Public and Its Problems* (albeit in reply to Walter Lippmann's *The Phantom Public* and for *Public Opinion*, Dewey pitched "The Great Community"). James Carey of Columbia University refers to *the public* as "the god-term of journalism—the be-all and end-all, the term without which the entire enterprise fails to make sense." David Mathews of the Kettering Foundation invokes *the public* in such works as *Is There a Public for Public Schools?* My argument to abandon the nominal public may not win the day; I may not persuade even myself. (Futile speculation, Dewey notes wryly, "is a companion of all philosophy".) I make the argument to clarify my thinking—and, if I argue well, perhaps yours—about what constitutes legitimate authority in a democracy. The argument sets out how The Public arises in political theory, elaborates from Dewey a justification of democracy that moves beyond public approval, and returns to the question of how we might better frame public matters in public discourse.

A brief history of the nominal public

Public comes into English from its origins as a Latin adjective, deriving from *res publica*, "public matters or things." *Publicus* may have been an emendation of *poplicus* (derived from the earlier *populus*, "people") as melded with *pubes*, "mature men," reflecting the age and gender requirements for citizenship in Rome.

The nominal public reflects older terms, such as the Greek *polis*, or "polity," the entity made up by the citizens of a city-state, such as Athens. The polis drew its authority from and imposed its authority upon the citizenry, which worked for those enfranchised because citizens and the city pursued a shared conceit of the good life. (Plato, nonetheless, dismissed the idea that people were sovereign.) But polis and res publica and popular sovereignty settled into a long winter's nap, as did all classical thinking, until dusted off by clerics in the Middle Ages. In the early 14th century, Marsilius of Padua reworked popular sovereignty to check papal authority and give more license to secular princes. But Marsilius was no populist. He placed authority to make laws on the "weightier part"—*valentior pars*—of the citizenry. When the princes had to be constrained, Locke conjured up as their usurper Natural Rights, which belonged to people individually but could be pooled to create—and, through rebellion, destroy—a state.

The Public's first big break came with the Enlightenment, when political authority came to be justified (somewhat paradoxically) as guaranteeing complete liberty to those who submitted themselves to it. That is expressed as Rousseau's "general will" and Kant's "good will" in the 18th century and T. H. Green's dictum in the 19th century: "Will, not force, is the basis of the state." This will is articulated by a sovereign people, aided by a legislator, in a kind of constitutional convention called whenever needed (Rousseau), or aggregated from individuals pursuing what's best for all (Kant), or expressed by custom (Green). As Peter P. Nicholson summarizes: "If laws are made by the general will, aimed at the common good and expressed by all the citizens, the laws must be in accordance with the public interest and therefore in the interest of each, and each is obliged by the law yet free because they are its author."

Most Enlightenment thinkers, writes J. S. McClelland:

> continued to think of democracy as the ancients did, as direct rule by the mob, the very antithesis of Reason, but Enlightenment did the job of ridiculing aristocratic claims to rule so well that when enlightened despotism failed there was no other direction for the theory of sovereignty to go than further down the road to a truly popularly exercised sovereignty. Out of this came the theory of the democratic republic.

That theory took a while to mature. "Democratic government had to wait a very long time before it could call itself democratic without blushing, so strong was the ancient idea that democracy was rule by the ignorant many," McClelland writes. "The enlightened compromise was government by representation." What should be represented? Property? Corporate communities? Individuals? Individuals won out eventually, "but that took two centuries of wrangling over what the principle of political representation truly meant."

Enlightenment theorizing became politics-on-the-ground in the American and French revolutions, with drastically different results. The American experiment exalted "We the People"—then defined *we* as "white male property owners," structured government to keep overheated majorities and overweening officeholders checked and balanced, and struggled for the next 200 years to realize more fully what We the People implied. In France, the journey from elevating the people as the Third Estate above the estates of kings and nobles to plunging the people into mob action and the Terror was over and done with in a decade (although government itself undulated on cyclical currents of empire, republic, and monarchy for the next 50 years).

The status of We the People has ebbed and flowed in the American experiment. "To follow the career of the term, *the People*, is to watch men invest a word with extraordinary meaning and then, losing hold of it to other claimants, scuttle from the consequences," Daniel T. Rodgers writes. Revolution-era citizens (white male property owners) were deferential to their betters, who let the people reign "but made sure they did not rule." In the early 19th century, the spread of democratic participation prompted the spread of literacy and plain speaking, and the age of Jacksonian democracy was born. "The crucial act of politics was no longer (as political theorists had always imagined it to be) that of governance or legislation but the reading of the popular will, when the people spoke at election," Rodgers writes. Not surprisingly, the first president to declare that he had been swept into office "by the will of the people" was Andrew Jackson.

By the mid-19th century, the People were being eclipsed by talk of state's rights and the rejection of the claims of women, free blacks, and slaves to be counted as People. Stephen Douglas tried and failed to make popular sovereignty the mechanism for resolving the sectional crisis over slavery. Abraham Lincoln could not keep the nation from the madness of civil war, but he was able to reassert the power of the Declaration of Independence and recast the whole purpose of the American experiment as "government by the people, of the people, for the people." Here was something, he offered in the Gettysburg Address that made slaughter bearable. Here were words that made Americans one people, dedicated to one proposition: self-government in a nation committed to the equality of its citizens.

The industrial proficiency that made the Civil War so bloody contributed to upheavals after the war and into the next century—and with it proclamations for and reactions against the rule of the People. The economically and politically marginalized asserted themselves as Populists and labor unionists and socialists, but the economically and politically powerful kept these People at bay. Early in the 20th century, the People became partners of the Progressives, but then were demoted to wards (some historians argue) as the Progressives embraced scientific management of human affairs. By the mid-20th century, the scientific measurement of public attitudes was perfected, and the scientific management of public opinion—born out of Freudian psychology, forged in propaganda during two world wars, fueled by commercial applications and now steered by polling—ascended to preeminence. The Public finally found its voice—or its ventriloquist.

Democratic legitimacy

So what does this history of The Public amount to? Much of it is drawn from McClelland, who observes:

> This history of political thought can be seen as the history of different legitimizing arguments for the state, and it may be that the democratic argument for legitimacy is the most powerful of all. Who, it might be asked, has the right to oppose what all have agreed to? Of course, this argument only applies to the

state *in general,* and it has very little to say about *government* and nothing at all to say about the day-to-day running of government.

John Dewey holds that most arguments over political legitimacy start at the wrong end. The contradictory theories of the state, "in spite of their divergence from one another, spring from a root of shared error: the taking of *causal agency* instead of *consequences* as the heart of the problem" (emphasis mine). Legitimacy of a political order does not arise from "state-forming forces" or other "direct causal factors." Legitimacy does not exist *a priori*—before political actors and political agents act. It arises *a posterior*—from the consequences of their actions. Contrary to arguments that start at the wrong end, a theory that starts with consequences focuses on the day-to-day running of government and other forms of democratic association in action.

Dewey's argument, though simple, breaks down into several steps he calls "matters of actual and ascertainable fact": All things (people included) act in association or combination with other things. The actions have results. Some results are noticed. Activities are undertaken "to secure consequences which are liked and eliminate those which are found obnoxious." Those affected have a common interest in the activities that produce or eliminate these consequences. In some cases, the consequences affect only those who, through their transactions, directly produce the consequences. In other cases, consequences affect others far beyond those immediately involved. Those directly affected but indirectly involved require some indirect means to control the activities that produce the consequences. "Now follows the hypothesis":

> Those indirectly and seriously affected for good or for evil form
> a group distinct enough to require recognition and a name.
> The name selected is The Public. This public is organized and
> made effective by means of representatives who as guardians
> of custom, as legislators, as executives, judges, etc., care for its
> especial interests by methods intended to regulate the conjoint

> actions of individuals and groups. Then and in so far association
> adds to itself political organization, and something which may
> be government comes into being, the public is a political state.

What does democracy offer The Public to help it "secure consequences which are liked and eliminate those which are found obnoxious"? I suggest three things:

- Efficacy. People achieve a sense of efficacy by sharing control of the means used to produce or avoid shared consequences. Hannah Arendt says that only by engaging in public life, in politics, can people fully realize their identity; otherwise they are obliterated as individuals by mass society. Efficacy matters. "The strength of families, communities, social institutions, and even nations lies partly in people's sense of collective efficacy that they can solve the problems they face and improve their lives through united effort," Albert Bandura writes. Democracy invites people to partake of public life, to realize their identities, to regulate "conjoint actions" affecting them.

- Epistemology/Education. Starting with Alexis de Tocqueville, many have argued that democracy is educative—it generates knowledge and the capacity to judge, which are required for good decisions by individuals and communities. As Dewey is at hand, I'll quote him: "The prime condition of a democratically organized public is a kind of knowledge and insight which does not yet exist"—until The Public called into being creates it. "In the absence of an articulate voice on the part of the masses, the best do not remain the best, the wise cease to be wise. It is impossible for high-brows to secure a monopoly of such knowledge as must be used for the regulation of common affairs." (F. A. Hayek offers the same justification for free enterprise.) "The strongest point to be made in behalf of even such rudimentary political forms as democracy has already attained, popular voting, majority rule, and so on, is that to some extent they involve a consultation and discussion which uncover social needs and troubles. . . .

The man who wears the shoe knows best that it pinches and where it pinches, even if the expert shoemaker is the best judge of how the trouble is to be remedied. . . . A class of experts is inevitably so removed from common interests as to become a class with private interests and private knowledge, which in social matters is not knowledge at all." Democracy invites people to share what they know, learn from others, form new insights and reach judgments that produce better consequences.

- Effectiveness. Effectiveness is a synergistic blend of efficacy and epistemology/education. Only when members of a political community feel a sense of personal efficacy and have a chance to discover and judge—to "work through," in Daniel Yankelovich's phrase—can truly effective action be taken. Otherwise, as champions of an action pursue it, others essential to its success will be passive at best and resistant at worst. Ronald A. Heifetz argues that the problems that most confound society require an adaptive response, which in turn requires learning about others' values, or reconciling dominant values with pressing realities, and then changing values, beliefs, or behaviors. That work must be done by the people who own the values, beliefs, and behaviors. Hannah Arendt and Mary Parker Follett argue that power comes from the capacity to act—to effect; implicitly, the greatest power comes from enabling the greatest number to act collaboratively. "Majority rule, just as majority rule, is as foolish as its critics charge it with being," Dewey writes. "But it never is *merely* majority rule. As a practical politician, Samuel J. Tilden, said a long time ago: 'The means by which a majority comes to be a majority is the more important thing': antecedent debates, modification of views to meet the opinions of minorities, the relative satisfaction given to the latter by the fact that it has had a chance and that next time it may be successful in becoming a majority." Democracy creates a greater capacity to act—and to act effectively.

Supplanting the nominal public with public work

Dewey makes his argument using *The Public* as a noun. David Mathews and others at Kettering write eloquently about the indefinite-article noun, *a public*, which comes into being to tackle a particular problem of common import. In other linguistic disputes, I generally side with the descriptivists, not the prescriptivists, and abjure policing usage. My argument against the nominal public most likely flunks Dewey's test for the justification of a system, because I cannot say my stance is of any consequence.

So perhaps I should be satisfied with the fact that the four English dictionaries I checked give nearly two to three times more definitions of *public* as an adjective than as a noun, and then quit the lists gracefully. Perhaps my real complaint is not with *The Public* as a noun, but with the verbs that precede or follow it.

Perhaps. But when I reread the transcript of *The Capital Gang*, I hear echoes of countless other public conversations by smart and thoughtful journalists, scholars, and researchers who frame The Public in the same way, letting the same veneer of omnipotent public opinion disguise a core empty of public judgment. It seems such a simple move to knock that chess piece, The Public, off the board in order to see how the game might otherwise proceed. For example, if claimants used *citizens* whenever they now default to *The Public*, the difficulties resulting from invoking the nominal public would be apparent. No one can claim that 100 percent of citizens support war; doing so invites contradiction, which begins a conversation or debate. Once a claimant begins making distinctions between which citizens do and which don't, then reflection, argument, social and political learning, and the search for the best solution can begin.

When a community or organization faces what Heifetz calls moments of disruptive disequilibrium, its members feel an urgent need to restore equilibrium by embracing quick answers offered by authoritative figures

—or by blaming the authorities for letting the rest down. Selling solutions or scapegoats by claiming concurrence of The Public does not improve the community's prospects for achieving the best consequence.

"Unless there are methods for detecting the energies which are at work and tracing them through an intricate network of interactions to their consequences, what passes as public opinion will be 'opinion' in its derogatory sense rather than truly public, no matter how widespread the opinion is," Dewey warns. "*Opinion casually formed* and formed under the direction of those who have something at stake in having a lie believed can be *public* opinion only in name"[1] (first emphasis mine; the second his).

And those who claim to have on their side The Public—or expertise, or God, or birthright, or might—are all making *a priori* claims to legitimacy. They are not engaging citizens, or experts, or spiritual communities, in a quest for the best course of action. They are not building citizens' sense of efficacy. They are not building new reservoirs of knowledge and judgment. They are not laying the groundwork for the sustained pursuit of an effective response. They are declaring victory and closing down the conversation. They are subverting public work. They are The Unpublic.

Instead of focusing on who The Public is or what The Public approves, what if we engaged in robust conversations about how public a political actor is being or how public a political action is? That, of course, would require continual discussions of what constitutes public action and why anyone should care. Each criterion, and what it takes to meet it, would be contested. Perhaps the ruckus would elbow citizens back into politics.

To start such a conversation, I offer the following criteria for evaluating political actors and their political actions. An action is public to the extent that it:

- Confers agency on, or acknowledges the agency of, citizens and citizens' designated agents, associations, or institutions.

- Helps the one, the many, and the whole—the individual, the associational (or social), and the communal—regulate activities whose consequences affect them.

- Embraces stewardship of common assets, liabilities, threats, and opportunities.

- Creates or sustains a shareable world, one in which associates and strangers alike can coordinate, cooperate, or compete/conflict with each other in constructive ways.

- Acknowledges other political actors, honors differences and similarities, and acts constructively on what is learned in interaction with others.

To illustrate with my field, news coverage would be considered public if it:

- Treats citizens as political actors (beyond voters or voters in waiting), seeking out their perspectives on public issues and producing, in collaboration with them, the knowledge and conceptual tools they require to be effective political actors.

- Identifies the stakes and stakeholders—those who act and those who are affected by the action—in public matters to help all assess consequences and regulate how the consequences are achieved.

- Pays attention to stuff that matters—the common assets, liabilities, threats, and opportunities that drive the well-being of citizens and communities.

- Covers coordination, cooperation, and conflict, focusing on how citizens and communities work through issues, reach public judgment, and undertake public work.

- Honors people's differences and similarities by reflecting the diversity of its communities; by not privileging certain classes of sources, subjects, or users, and by adapting practices based on what the journalists learn from critics, fans, and anyone else.

What constitutes public action in your work with politics, philosophy, and public policy? Would more public action in your field bring more citizens into politics? Should anyone care? Let the ruckus begin.

General Sources

Arendt, Hannah. *The Human Condition*. Chicago: University of Chicago Press, 1958.

Boyte, Harry C., and Nancy N. Kari. *Building America: The Democratic Process of Public Work*. Philadelphia: Temple University Press, 1996.

Caspary, William R. *Dewey on Democracy*. Ithaca, NY: Cornell University Press, 2000.

Ewen, Stuart. *PR! A Social History of Spin*. New York: Basic Books, 1996.

Graham, Pauline, ed. *Mary Parker Follett—Prophet of Management: A Celebration of Writings from the 1920s*. Boston: Harvard Business School Press, 1995.

Hayek, F. A. *The Road to Serfdom*. Chicago: University of Chicago Press, 1944.

Heifetz, Ronald A. *Leadership Without Easy Answers*. Cambridge, MA: Belknap Press, 1994.

Lasch, Christopher. *The Revolt of the Elites and the Betrayal of American Democracy*. New York: Norton, 1995.

Lippmann, Walter. *Public Opinion*. New York: Free Press Paperbacks, 1922, 1997 edition.

———. *The Phantom Public*. New York: Library of Conservative Thought, 1925, 1993 reprint.

Mathews, David. *Is There a Public for Public Schools?* Dayton, OH: Kettering Foundation Press, 1996.

———. *Politics for People: Finding a Responsible Public Voice*. Urbana, IL: University of Illinois Press, second edition, 1994, 1999.

McGowan, John. *Hannah Arendt: An Introduction*. Minneapolis, MN: University of Minnesota Press, 1998.

Schudson, Michael. *The Good Citizen: A History of American Civic Life*. New York: Free Press, 1998.

Wiebe, Robert H. *Self-Rule: A Cultural History of American Democracy*. Chicago: University of Chicago Press, 1995.

Wills, Garry. *Lincoln at Gettysburg: The Words that Remade America*. New York: Touchstone, 1992.

Yankelovich, Daniel. *Coming to Public Judgment: Making Democracy Work in a Complex World*. Syracuse, NY: Syracuse University Press, 1991.

———. *The Magic of Dialogue: Transforming Conflict into Cooperation*. New York: Simon & Schuster, 1999.

Sources on Citizen Alienation from Politics

Bauman, Zygmunt. *In Search of Politics.* Stanford, CA: Stanford University Press, 1999.

Boggs, Carl. *The End of Politics: Corporate Power and the Decline of the Public Sphere.* New York: Guilford Press, 2000.

Doppelt, Jack C., and Ellen Shearer. *Nonvoters: America's No-Shows.* Thousand Oaks, CA: Sage, 1999.

Eliasoph, Nina. *Avoiding Politics: How Americans Produce Apathy in Everyday Life.* Cambridge: Cambridge University Press, 1998.

Entman, Robert M. *Democracy Without Citizens: Media and the Decay of American Politics.* New York: Oxford University Press, 1989.

Johnson, Dennis W. *No Place for Amateurs: How Political Consultants are Reshaping American Democracy.* London: Routledge, 2001.

Piven, Frances Fox, and Richard A. Cloward. *Why Americans Still Don't Vote: And Why Politicians Want It That Way.* Boston: Beacon Press, 2000.

Putnam, Robert D. *Bowling Alone: The Collapse and Revival of American Community.* New York: Simon & Schuster, 2000.

Skocpol, Theda, and Morris P. Fiorina, eds. *Civic Engagement in American Democracy.* Washington/New York: Brookings Institution Press/Russell Sage Foundation, 1999.

Schier, Steven E. *By Invitation Only: The Rise of Exclusive Politics in the United States.* Pittsburgh, PA: University of Pittsburgh Press, 2000.

Snyder, R. Claire. *Shutting the Public Out of Politics: Civic Republicanism, Professional Politics, and the Eclipse of Civil Society.* Dayton, OH: Occasional Paper of the Kettering Foundation, 1999.

Dictionaries

The Compact Edition of the Oxford English Dictionary, vol. II. Oxford: Oxford University Press, 1971.

The American Heritage Dictionary of the English Language. Boston: Houghton Mifflin, 2000.

Webster's New World College Dictionary. New York: Macmillan, 1996.

Webster's II New College Dictionary. Boston, Houghton Mifflin, 1995.

JOURNALISM'S
MORAL AUTHORITY

In two essays several years apart, Cole grappled
with journalism's role as a warning beacon
on significant threats that called for public action.
In this piece, written not long after 9/11,
Cole boldly tackled a difficult subject and strove
to place it in the context of journalism's larger
challenges. In the next, longer essay, he expanded
on that theme in the wake of Hurricane Katrina.

JOURNALISTS HAVE DONE much to be proud of in the wake of the September 11 attacks. The staff of the *Wall Street Journal* covered terrorism at the *Journal's* front door, and reporters and photographers in New York risked their lives on the streets around the World Trade Center. Across the country, newsrooms responded with extra editions, special broadcasts, and continuous web updates. The coverage has been detailed and sweeping in scope. The nation has needed saturation coverage to comprehend, and bear, the unbearable losses. Journalism has reasserted its genuine value in a time of crisis.

But the conversation about what news organizations could have done to lessen the nation's vulnerability to attack cannot be avoided. Important questions have been raised—and the way we respond will say important things about how we see our work.

Reading Jim Romenesko's *MediaNews*, the outlines of the conversation are already emerging. It's evident in several recent postings, beginning with Geneva Overholser's lucid summary of the basic indictment.

"Many have asked, 'How could our intelligence services have failed us so?' But I would ask: 'How could our reporting on intelligence have been so poor?'" Overholser writes:

In February, CIA Director George Tenet told the Senate Intelligence Committee that Osama bin Laden's "global network" was the "most immediate and serious" terrorist threat to the United States. A handful of newspapers covered the testimony, and even their stories were brief and buried.

A few weeks before that, a bipartisan commission released a report saying "the relative invulnerability of the US homeland to catastrophic attack" was coming to an end. The commission, headed by former Sens. Gary Hart and Warren Rudman, said, "A direct attack against American citizens on American soil is likely over the next quarter-century." The report hardly was noticed. The *New York Times* didn't cover it.

Overholser cites a precipitous drop in international coverage, driven by expense, a misreading of public interest in world news and a fixation on local news. Then she quotes former *Times* reporter Leslie Gelb, who served on the bipartisan commission:

It is a failure to report on substance. I would say the biggest problem for people in public policy schools or think tanks is to get any coverage of the substantive work being done. . . . Most of the stories have nothing to do with policy. Almost all are about politics: "She says; he says." It is horrific.

John Balzar, a columnist at the *Los Angeles Times*, defends the journalism profession in the person of his colleague, John-Thor Dahlburg, citing Dahlburg's stories that have run on Page One of the *Los Angeles Times* over the past several years.

"Dahlburg, of course, wasn't the only foreign correspondent to see attacks coming. But for my money, no one did a better job of it. Over and over again, for years now, he has been sounding warnings. He explained the motive and the means and predicted the timing," Balzar writes. "If you could have pleaded this evidence in court, I doubt that any judge in the country would have refused a restraining order against the Taliban. It was that clear and convincing and, we now know, horribly provident."

"If anyone is to blame for an intelligence failure, it is us, the stakeholders in our democracy," Balzar concludes. "And, of course, those we elect to serve us."

Of course, the *Los Angeles Times* is an exceptional newspaper, one of four that employ more than two-thirds of the nation's newspaper foreign correspondents, as noted by Stephen Ponder, a journalism professor at the University of Oregon. Ponder says the overall lack of context "may have contributed to the shock felt by Americans when they abruptly found themselves on the front lines of international terrorism."

At the same time, Ponder faults news consumers and worries that they may "once again turn inward, as they did after 1991 [after the Persian Gulf War], and fail to demand that their news media help them to understand the world they ignore at their peril." Caryl Rivers, a journalism professor at Boston University, hopes that, given the exceptional coverage of terrorism's aftermath, "Maybe, just maybe, consumers will get used to this kind of quality, and demand more of it."

There seem to be three fundamental questions that can be asked about journalism in general, as well as journalism assessing the threat of terrorism.

• *Do news organizations help citizens and communities, including political leaders, identify and respond to the most significant threats to well-being?*

Increasingly, journalism has been accused of being a source of distraction rather than a tool of attentiveness, and not just because of its growing obsession with scandal and celebrity. The litany of charges is familiar: Americans' disproportionate fear of crime reflects disproportionate crime coverage. Americans' rank ordering of threats to life and limb overstates dangers that journalists consider newsworthy and understates deadlier, but less newsworthy, conditions. Americans' grasp of scientific issues—threats to the environment, risks of genetic engineering—is muddied by coverage that frames them as disputes over who calls the shots in regulatory schemes. Americans' sense of responsibility for global suffering is eroded by "compassion fatigue" from too many heartwrenching depictions and too few explanations of what might be done.

At the purely local level, does your news organization consistently and realistically identify the threats—economic, environmental, health, criminal, and so on—that your communities face? Or is such coverage reactive—swinging into high gear only after a horrible incident, or after a politician or activist group makes a big deal of an issue?

• *Do news organizations pursue a well-grounded definition of what constitutes substantive coverage?*

In *The Elements of Journalism*, Bill Kovach and Tom Rosenstiel set out admirable standards, such as pursuing truth, serving citizens, verifying facts, maintaining independence, monitoring power, providing forums, exercising conscience. Their take on making the significant "interesting and relevant" deals mostly with storytelling forms, while keeping the news "comprehensive and proportional" deals with overstatement and niche marketing. We could use clearer standards of how to focus on what truly matters.

If our definition of substantive journalism is too narrow, we risk being entirely substantive and yet still irrelevant to the concerns of people or the threats confronting them. For example: Coverage of the apparatus and workings of power in politics can be quite substantive, but it omits a wide range of equally substantive topics, such as the policies contemplated, the uncertainties of success (not political success, but operational success), the limitations of knowledge shaping all public choice, and so on.

• *Do news organizations take responsibility for how their work is pursued and how it is received?*

This is a most troubling question—and one that underlies, or undermines, the answers to all others. The conversation emerging in *MediaNews* reflects the reflexive ways we assign responsibility to others: political authorities who focus on domestic priorities but not international ones or who fail to signal the significance of a report or even "shut it down"; owners more interested in cutting costs than in covering news; a culture that has wrapped itself in a "national fog of materialism and disinterest and avoidance"; audiences that don't care, and worse, don't demand enough of us.

These notions are not atypical. Substantive research has documented that journalists and sources routinely negotiate over what's news—over the balance of interest vs. importance required to turn a report, a hearing, a claim into a story or photo. At a meeting of the Association for Education in Journalism and Mass Communication convention, some members of the opening keynote panel wished out loud that audiences better appreciated journalists and quality journalism. And one panelist— Michael Gartner, Pulitzer laureate, former president of the American Society of Newspaper Editors and of NBC News—proposed journalism education not for prospective journalists but for citizens, so they can arm themselves against shoddy work. And the body of journalistic commentary blaming owners for every journalistic shortcoming is burgeoning.

We journalists need a stronger sense of moral agency than that. We need to ratchet up our journalism-ethics discussions to encompass journalism's moral authority. The preceding three questions point to one underlying query: Does journalism have a sense of its moral responsibility and a commitment to discharge it?

We journalists must take responsibility for making substantive journalism about real risks *salient*—to use Dave Poltrack's term—to our sources, owners, and users. Poltrack, a CBS executive, uses *salient* in a psychological sense—perceiving something as relevant to one's life. That's useful, but insufficient. In moral journalism, *salient* is more than important, interesting, or relevant. It's more than selling a story that no one would otherwise read, or dumping it on the world with a righteous claim it *ought* to be read. For journalists, *salient* is a moral term, not a marketing one. Its Latin root, *salire*, means "to leap out." So *salient* also means "protruding, strikingly conspicuous, prominent." Our moral responsibility is to cover significant threats to well-being, substantively, in such a way that our coverage leaps out, protrudes, and is strikingly and conspicuously prominent. So that it sears the conscience of our fellow citizens. Exceptions—a talented foreign correspondent here, a few Page-One stories there—cannot do that for a nation. It takes a profession.

Newspapers know how to make stories that they deem important salient to their readers—and to the public officials responsible for the ills they uncover. Consider "Gateway to Gridlock," the *Chicago Tribune*'s series on airport delays. The *Tribune* sent reporters to seven airports and five control towers to report on one day in the life of air travel in America. A total of 26 reporters contributed, and their reports ran over several full pages for four days. *Chicago* magazine described the series as "packed with literary detail and a dash of investigative oomph." The Pulitzer board described it as a "clear and compelling profile of the chaotic American air traffic system." The series won the 2001 Pulitzer Prize for explanatory reporting.

Airport delays are important to business and leisure travelers, so maybe it did not require too much literary detail and investigative dash to make the series salient to readers and regulators. Still, after September 11, one has to wonder: What if the series—with the same resources, the same depth, the same conspicuous prominence—had focused its explanatory power on the chaotic American airport security system?

Newspapers at times have blown their obligation to make an important unfolding story salient. Laurel Leff of Northeastern University has analyzed the *New York Times'* coverage of the Holocaust, from 1939 to 1945 (published in Harvard's *International Journal of Press/Politics,* Spring 2000). Her conclusion:

> The placement of news about the Holocaust almost uniformly on inside pages, as well as the failure to highlight it in editorials or in summaries of important events, made it difficult for most Americans to find the facts and to understand their importance ... despite the detailed, credible information that was available, the American public actually did not know about the Holocaust while it was happening because mainstream American news-papers never presented the story of the extermination of the Jews in a way that highlighted its importance.

In other words, the *Times* had the story. It just didn't make it salient.

One of my heroes in our profession is Arthur Sulzberger Jr., the *Times'* publisher, because of his commitment to quality journalism *and* his business vision. He told a journalism class at Columbia University that one of the biggest failures in the *Times'* 150-year history was not alerting the world to the Holocaust's atrocities.

He understands the moral dimension of salience in journalism.

Substance without salience is pontificating. Salience without substance is pandering. Consistent and realistic coverage of the most significant threats to well-being (and opportunities to improve it) is the primary purpose of journalism. That's what makes journalism a worthy calling—and a moral one.

Journalism and Public Knowledge

B ILL MCKIBBEN, the environmental writer, offered in the *New York Reiew of Books* this bracing summary of what's missing in America's current political order:

> The technology we need most badly is the technology of community—the knowledge about how to cooperate to get things done. Our sense of community is in disrepair at least in part because the prosperity that flowed from cheap fossil fuel has allowed us all to become extremely individualized, even hyperindividualized, in ways that, as we only now begin to understand, represent a truly Faustian bargain. Americans haven't needed our neighbors for anything important, and hence neighborliness—local solidarity—has disappeared. Our problem now is that there is no way forward, at least if we're serious about preventing the worst ecological nightmares, that doesn't involve working together politically to make changes deep enough and rapid enough to matter.

While McKibben's assigned topic is environmental catastrophe, his analysis applies equally to the whole range of intractable social problems. If we want to make progress in tackling war, crime, poverty, educational achievement, health-care costs, and similarly contested issues, we need new ways of understanding and acting on them collectively, as publics. This directly implicates those of us who work within institutions and professions, because institutions and professions are in themselves community technologies.

Unfortunately, institutions and professions seem rather to have taken upon themselves the role of guardians—specially trained folks trying to guide and direct citizens about what's best for them. They see themselves as working *for* the public rather than *with* the public. The first approach, working *for* a public, casts citizens as clients, consumers, dependents; the second, working *with* a public, casts them as collaborators, cocreators of value, actual sovereigns. The first approach is what Immanuel Kant, in 1784, called "tutelage," a grave threat to freedom. "Tutelage," Kant wrote, "is man's inability to make use of his understanding without guidance from another."

The thoughts that follow are offered in terms of journalism and journalistic enterprises, the institutional and professional domain I know best. Yet they will apply, I suspect, to most if not all institutions and professions. In thinking about how journalism can function better as a technology of community rather than a technology of tutelage, the primary questions, as I see them, are, how do communities recognize and respond to common challenges or opportunities? how might they recognize and respond more effectively? Corollary questions, then, inevitably follow: how does journalism help communities recognize and respond to common challenges and opportunities? how might it do so more effectively?

Some practitioners are beginning to think of themselves as democratic professionals, according to political scientist Albert Dzur of Bowling Green State University. Professionals have key civic roles to play and must contribute more to public life than skilled expertise. Dzur's studies of professionals in criminal justice, medicine, and journalism indicate that they share civic and professional tasks with citizens. Just as police officers often think of themselves as the "thin blue line" between order and chaos, between the people they serve and the criminal element they suppress, journalists often think of themselves as the go-betweens—between citizens and public life.

But in a democracy, practitioners and professionals function best as catalysts and facilitators of public acting, not as go-betweens. Police departments that embrace community policing, work closely with citizens to identify the most pressing priorities for public safety, the work that citizens can do best and the work that trained professionals can do best. Journalists that help *form* publics as well as *inform* publics also begin to see their skill sets as assets to share rather than as grounds to supplant citizens in deciding what a community should pay attention to. Journalists can help citizens generate and share insights into what their community should address.

The dominant model in journalism is the trustee, or transmission, model. This model casts journalists in the role of trustees who transmit knowledge from other guardians to citizens, whose lives may be affected by it. Traditional journalism thus assumes a professional practice, based on trained reporters and editors, who find authoritative information and communicate it authoritatively to the public. A journalist finds the experts who know what is (or ought to be) happening; the journalist then extracts what the experts know and transmits this knowledge to everybody else. Sometimes, indeed, the knowledge transmitted is about the guardian who is its primary source—Walter Lippmann's conceit of the "hot glare of publicity," which allows people as voters to throw the rascals out if the guardians go too far in advancing their own interests ahead of the public interest. Like other professionals, the journalist bears a truth that can and sometimes should affect citizens' actions.

In the trustee/transmission model, journalism's primary function is to secure and disseminate information—"the best obtainable version of the truth," to use an axiom popularized by journalists Carl Bernstein and Bob Woodward of Watergate fame. This kind of journalism is genuinely valuable.

The aftermath of the drowning of New Orleans by Hurricane Katrina shows that journalism matters profoundly when people and communities find themselves in catastrophic circumstances. The 2006 Pulitzer Prize for Public Service went to two Gulf Coast newspapers for their coverage of the storm. The *Sun-Herald* of Gulfport-Biloxi, Mississippi, won "for its valorous and comprehensive coverage of Hurricane Katrina, providing a lifeline for devastated readers, in print and online, during their time of greatest need." The *Times-Picayune* was recognized "for its heroic, multifaceted coverage of Hurricane Katrina and its aftermath, making exceptional use of the newspaper's resources to serve an inundated city even after evacuation of the newspaper plant."

But the destruction also throws into sharp relief other critical questions about the trustee/transmission model. The model presumes that someone always knows the truth about complex issues, and the public interest is served when journalists faithfully fulfill their role in transmitting expert truth to the public. But when it comes to helping communities avoid calamities, such as Hurricane Katrina, that presumption may not bear out. Does journalism matter when it comes to averting disaster? Can journalism help communities *avoid* catastrophe by calling people to act as citizens and reach judgments as a public? In an era of information overload and fragmented publics, can journalists direct sustained attention to critical issues until they are resolved?

The trustee/transmission model says journalists are innocent of what happens after we sound the clarion call because action belongs to others. This is the thrust of Tim Rutten's analysis in the *Los Angeles Times* published September 2, 2005:

> Three years ago, New Orleans' leading local newspaper, the *Times-Picayune*, National Public Radio's signature nightly news program, *All Things Considered*, and the *New York Times* each methodically and compellingly reported that the very existence of south Louisiana's leading city was at risk and hundreds of thousands of lives imperiled by exactly the sequence of events that occurred this week. All three news organizations also made clear that the danger was growing because of a series of public policy decisions and failure to allocate government funds to alleviate the danger. . . . Politics may have failed the

people of New Orleans. Politicians certainly failed them. They may have failed themselves by not demanding better. But their newspaper and other important segments of the American press did not fail them.

Rutten's analysis makes sense if we conceive of journalism's work as "warn and scorn": Warn people about possible catastrophe, then heap scorn upon those who fail to heed us. Yet if we offer prophecies that no one believes (the proof of belief being the willingness to act on it), then we are nothing more than modern-day Cassandras, peddling prophecies with no social utility. We can take no solace in a supposed moral virtue. For when our communities are destroyed, so is our lifeblood as news organizations. So are our homes.

In the *New York Times* of the same date, Mark Fischetti, a contributing editor for *Scientific American*, described a major push that brought together "all the parties to one table in 1998 and got them to agree on a coordinated solution" with a price tag of $14 billion, about twice the amount appropriated for a major public works project to resuscitate the Florida Everglades. But conflicting priorities in Congress and Louisiana meant that "the magic moment of consensus was lost. Thus, in true American fashion, we ignored an inevitable problem until disaster focused our attention."

Does *inevitable* inevitably mean "unavoidable"? Is "true American fashion" a cultural straitjacket from which we cannot escape? In the case of New Orleans, the costs of taking action and the costs of not acting were both known. What was unknown was when a catastrophic hurricane might hit. Therefore there was no "best obtainable version of the truth" about how aggressively public agencies should reinforce levees or take other expensive steps to mitigate such a potential catastrophe. In hindsight, after the devastation of Hurricane Katrina, we can say the cost of reconstruction will be several orders of magnitude higher than would have been the cost of preparedness. But to make the best judgment in a situation of uncertainty about when bad things might happen requires more than expertise. It requires judgment. This kind of judgment requires a different kind of journalism.

Despite all that was known about the threat to New Orleans, the larger *polis* did not act in a way adequate to avert catastrophe. Can we imagine a new kind of journalism, a new relationship of the profession to the public that would equip citizens and their communities to come to sound judgment on such issues before catastrophe strikes? The goal of such a new model of journalism must be to engage people in imagining the future they want and in analyzing possible approaches that might achieve that future. Rather than settle for transmitting expert or elite knowledge, it will aim to generate "public knowledge," produced by a public's use of reason and experience.

Knowledge, in this usage, is not a commodity that can be stored up and transmitted as needed; rather, this is a kind of knowledge constantly being generated by—and in turn generating—new insights among citizens, experts, and elites working with each other as a community. To the extent that the expertise and knowledge of the press and of other professionals can serve in generating this *public* knowledge, such professionals are valuable instrumental members of the community.

Public knowledge thus defined includes:

- Knowledge that is already dispersed (if latent) among people and their institutions, which can be made accessible to, assessable by, and usable by all.

- Knowledge known to specialists that can be dispersed so people and institutions can put it to collective use, particularly in reaching public judgment.

- Knowledge that is created and shared by people and institutions when they collaborate in the public sphere.

- Knowledge that is creatable, sharable, and actionable *only* in public—only by taking part, by taking action, in the public sphere.

How, then, is public knowledge generated? How does it generate, among the public, a will and capacity to act? There are five clusters of activities that drive public knowledge. Ideally and theoretically, they happen in sequence; in reality, they may overlap, stall, or loop back on themselves as new information is made available:

Myth and meaning. Communities—indeed, organizations and associations of all shapes, sizes, and scales—develop myths about themselves and their capacities to act. When a patriarch exhorts family members to "remember who you are and how we Campbells do things," he is invoking a family myth to guide individual and collective actions by family members. Even state seals and mottoes speak to dominant myths, such as wizened skepticism (Missouri is the "Show Me" state) or virtuous vigilance against usurpers of popular sovereignty (Virginia displays an armed Virtue astride a prostrate tyrant on its state shield). Richard Harwood of the Harwood Institute for Public Innovation says that beleaguered communities can rise to meet the challenges facing them only when they fashion a new story, a new myth, about their aspirations and capacities. Myths inform the frameworks people use to make sense and meaning out of specific events, acts, and incidents. Myths shape how we create meaning out of Hurricane Katrina's catastrophic impact or out of the September 11, 2001, attacks on New York and Washington.

Surveillance and assessment. Through institutions and professions, sometimes through citizens acting in concert, communities pay attention to what's happening in order to respond appropriately. They undertake community versions of corporate environmental scans and SWOT analyses—that is, analyzing how the community's strengths and weaknesses position it to respond to opportunities and threats. Sometimes this entails formal "visioning" sessions or long-term planning for highways or economic development strategies. Often it is more informal, percolating in barbershops and dinner conversations and coffee klatches.

Public discourse. Then communities begin to talk about what might be done about opportunities and threats, how strengths can be leveraged and weaknesses mitigated. Public discourse is not typified by *how* people talk—high oratory or stentorian intonations—but by what is talked about and what shapes the talk. Elements that make up public discourse, or shape it, include: data-driven descriptions of current, historical, or foreseeable conditions; aspirations, values, and experiences from individual lives; options, consequences, trade-offs, and uncertainty; and, stakes, interests, and differential power within the community.

Public judgment. Public discourse begins to take on a power for sustained action through something like the process of public judgment as articulated by Daniel Yankelovich, the polling pioneer, and cofounder of Public Agenda. The process, as he describes it, entails three main phases: consciousness raising, which pulls data from surveillance and assessment activities to direct general public attention to a particular issue; working through choices and trade-offs; and reaching resolution about which choices offer the best course of action. He explains that these movements of a public mind may take months, years, or sometimes generations for a people fully to work through.

Public work. Finally, the community translates its judgment into action, and assesses and revises that action based on its experience. Public work can be done by institutions and professions—in fact, it ought to be demanded of them—but it transcends experts and elites. Public work, as Harry Boyte of the University of Minnesota reminds us, is the work we do in common; it is the work that makes us citizens; it is the work of a *public*. As David Mathews, president of the Kettering Foundation, explains in his historical analyses of public education in America, the public schools were born literally of public work, citizens raising their own money and raising the walls of their own schools, and need to be sustained and nurtured to this day through public work, the direct engagement of citizens with institutions of teaching and learning. Public work is seen in the continuing exercise of a collective, or public, will, and it has space for the individual, the community institution, and the professional organization alike.

129

This system of public knowledge is empirical in that it is observable, but it is not inevitable. In other words, to borrow from appreciative inquiry, this synopsis describes the system when the process works best. I describe these clusters as cyclically linear, in that one cluster of activities is usually an antecedent to others and the cycle renews itself when public work helps reshape public myth and meaning. But there are clearly instances when the sequence is not followed and, in fact, may be reversed. Multiple factors can disrupt or suboptimize public knowledge. In fact, the continuing challenge to institutions and professions committed to effective democratic practice is to think through how their own practices advance or subvert the process of public knowledge. How can we make the process of public knowledge both normal and normative and not exceptional?

At the Reynolds School of Journalism at the University of Nevada, Reno, we are undertaking an experiment in reconceiving journalism as a social practice, as a mediating institution in the generation of public knowledge. I describe the experiment here to illustrate by one example, in practical terms, how this public knowledge model can guide professional and institutional practice.

We are running a 10-month, intensive master's program enrolling journalists and working with Nevada and California news enterprises. In this program, journalists are experimenting with interactive media tools that connect citizens, experts, and elites in discussing environmental policy and the Lake Tahoe Basin. Lake Tahoe is a beautiful lake, nestled in the Alpine forests atop the Sierra Nevada range. As the Tahoe Basin has developed into a tourist and second-home paradise, natural wildfires have been suppressed and stringent land-use regulations have been imposed to protect the lake from runoff, which decreases its clarity. Yet some of the land-use regulations, such as those limiting the removal of trees from property, actually aggravate the risk of wildfire. The people who live and work and visit the lake are divided among two states, multiple residential communities, and a host of governmental and regulatory jurisdictions. While not commensurate with the loss of New Orleans as a functional city, the potential for wildfire at Lake Tahoe presents a similar, smaller scale case study. The threat was sketched by Don Thompson of the Associated Press in a report published in 2005:

> Scenic, wooded Lake Tahoe, one of America's natural gems, could easily go up in smoke, speakers at an annual lakeside summit warned Sunday. Much of the attention—and millions of dollars—have gone in recent years to protecting the high alpine lake's fabled clear blue waters, where visibility once penetrated to more than 100 feet and has recently been improving.
>
> But it is the forested Sierra Nevada mountains reflected in the lake that could destroy the basin that is home to multimillion dollar homes, casinos, ski resorts, lodges, restaurants, and parks that draw thousands of tourists. Moreover, a fast-moving wildfire on a crowded summer weekend could pose deadly danger to panicked people fleeing over the Tahoe basin's few winding roads. . . .
>
> "If there was a fire to happen here, it wouldn't matter how much we spent to keep Tahoe blue—because it wouldn't be blue," said Bruce Kranz, a member of the Placer County, Calif. Board of Supervisors. Scientists say such a wildfire could set back lake restoration efforts by 100 years.

And so our cohort of journalists is developing a web-based publishing program designed to connect all these constituents as collaborators to weigh what is—and what ought to be—happening in the Lake Tahoe Basin. The journalists are developing web pages to help people explore myths and meanings about the lake, to survey and assess threats to the lake, and to discuss alternative approaches to protecting it, thus working toward public judgment about appropriate policies and shared work to protect the lake. The journalists are developing narratives to help raise the consciousness of everyone who cares about the lake—and they are inviting citizens to share their own stories about why and how the lake matters to them. They are developing web pages to pull together agency agendas, scientific and policy expertise, elite perspectives, and citizen perspectives. They are developing pages to foster dialogue and deliberation about the trade-offs involved in protecting water clarity as distinct from reducing wildfire risks. One project, Promise Tahoe, makes it easy for citizens to invite one another to join in specific public work tasks to protect the lake.

In doing this work, these journalists are filling a variety of roles that transcend the normal notion of a journalist as a synthesizer of public meetings, diviner of public documents and databases, or an interviewer of notable figures. They are acting as mapmakers, laying out the policy—and actual terrain. They are acting as candid friends, offering honest feedback to citizens, experts, and elites. They are storytellers, helping capture the lake's essence through image and narrative. They are impresarios, inviting citizens, experts, and elites to share their stories and pool their knowledge. They are mediators and facilitators of public conversation and deliberation. And they are mindful inquisitors, using photography, cartography, geographic information systems, computer animation, audio, video, and good-old text to inquire about what's happening in the Tahoe Basin and to encourage citizens to imagine what they want to see happening there.

All this experimentation is grounded on a detailed examination of current journalistic practice, and imagines new journalistic practices that better reflect what it takes for democracy to go well. A principal source of insight is the work of John Dewey. Dewey argued that members of a community, working together, are capable of governing themselves. The problems of modern democracy, in this understanding, do not lie in the people themselves, but in the institutions and professions that serve them poorly. Institutions and professions should cast themselves as agents *of the people*, not agencies working *on behalf* of the people. They should perceive and engage citizens as political actors, not as clients and consumers. In investigating what should be done about common problems, the processes of inquiry, whether journalistic, legislative, or executive, should invite all stakeholders—citizen, expert, and elite—to speak and to act. Inquiry should be considered contingent and open to revision, as more about any particular problem or opportunity is experienced and learned. Accountability, a goal of all journalism, should be imposed on citizens for what happens in their communities, on institutions and professions for how they act as citizens' agents, and on journalists as mediators between citizens, experts, and elites.

In *First Democracy*, Paul Woodruff of the University of Texas considers Athens' 200-year experiment with self-government. He neither fawns over, nor demonizes, Athenian democracy. Instead, he considers its strengths and weaknesses, and particularly Athenians' continuous efforts to strengthen their democracy. He extracts a simple but profound framework for what it takes for democracy to work well. It echoes Dewey's work. These are the seven essential elements in Woodruff's framework:

- Freedom from tyranny (and from being a tyrant)
- Harmony
- The rule of law
- Natural equality
- Citizen wisdom
- Reasoning without knowledge
- Education

The first four elements are fundamental to creating what we now call "social capital"—the personal and institutional capacity of community members to work with people like themselves and unlike themselves. These four elements embody a simple idea: we must be unencumbered (free from tyranny, deep divisions, lawlessness, and unequal standing) in order to collaborate in self-rule.

The final four elements (for natural equality belongs in both sets) are fundamental to generating what Dewey called "social intelligence"— the personal and institutional capacity of community members to generate insights about what the community must do to secure good consequences and avoid bad ones. This intelligence is generated through the synthesis of experiences, ideas, interests, values, and aspirations with facts or data or information. And these four elements embody a second simple idea: we must share our insights in order to chart our best course as a community.

Woodruff illuminates the entire framework of democracy with this observation: "The outcome of most public decisions cannot be known in advance. . . . The future—even the near future—is unknown to us." Dewey, too, argued that the contingent nature of decisions, the unknowable future, is a profound reason that we need democracy. We need full access to the wisdom distributed throughout the community to make the best guess at the best course. We need to test our collective thinking. We must minimize forces that disrupt generating and testing wisdom—self-serving tyrants, or factions, or lawless chaos—so that everyone's knowledge can be shared and evaluated.

We need the greatest investment in public knowledge so that, as a community, we can nimbly adjust and adapt as things play out differently than expected. And that's why we need institutions and professions that take themselves seriously as community technologies—willing to examine their practices, experiment with new ones, and adapt to the ever-changing conditions, as they become manifest in a shared understanding of the dilemmas that we face as a people.

MEANING AND CONNECTION

*Cole wrote several essays about the possibilities ahead
for journalism schools. Those essays, which often referenced
specific schools, are adapted here to reflect his thinking
on the responsibilities and opportunities for journalism
education in the early 21st century.*

I N ERROL MORRIS' DOCUMENTARY FILM *The Fog of War*, Robert
McNamara relates a story from his days as an assistant professor at
Harvard Business School, following the attack on Pearl Harbor. As young
men were pouring into the armed services, the business school faced the
prospect of closing its doors for the duration of the war. The school did
suspend civilian instruction from 1943 to 1945, but instead of closing,
Dean Donald K. David started the Advanced Management Program to
train military officers. He did not wait for the War Department to come
to him. He anticipated what an officer corps might need to know about
managing forces in a time of global conflagration and he supplied it. The
Advanced Management Program became the cornerstone of Harvard's
executive education programs, which have trained more than 45,000
business leaders from around the world.

While we are not in a situation as dire as a world war, journalism,
advertising, and other media ventures are in the midst of massive dis-
locations. And the world we serve is beset by warfare, globalization,
technological disruptions, political and social revolutions, and economic uncertainties. For journalism schools, all this presents a substantial
opportunity to invent approaches that can transform journalism educa
tion. Several broad areas are worth exploring.

Mastering change: purposeful journalism and adaptive innovation

During periods of upheaval, people and organizations suffer anxiety about what they must surrender in order to survive or advance. They cling to outmoded practices and routines because they see them as embodiments of their larger purpose and of their professional identity. They may scapegoat colleagues who experiment with alternative practices, fearing that these colleagues are undermining the profession. In seeking to explain problems in their domain, they focus on a few people who violate professional norms—rather than consider any shortcomings in the domain's dominant paradigm. Sometimes fundamentalist movements arise to codify current conventions as the epitome of professional standards, confusing what must endure with what must be dynamic.

And so, in recent years we have witnessed heated debates over public journalism, tremendous attention paid to malfeasants, such as Jayson Blair, and the impressive efforts of the Committee of Concerned Journalists and the Project on Excellence in Journalism to focus attention on affirming professional standards. (The committee also seeks to secure consumer demand and corporate support for such standards.) There is much of value in these debates, cases, and standards. But there also is opportunity to enrich these conversations by judging journalism's practices against its purpose and by directing attention to external forces that drive change and internal forces that resist innovation.

Given the upheavals in the world of journalism, advertising, and communication, a journalism school can take advantage of a number of possibilities for research, teaching, and service. Some examples:

- Purpose as a programmatic emphasis. Journalism's purpose is the foundation that secures it against tumult. But we rarely reflect on our purpose—or study how our craft disciplines, tools, and practices serve or undermine it. What does journalism aim to accomplish? Journalism education can infuse courses and programs with referents to purpose (alongside ethics and technology) and convene scholars and practitioners in a national conversation about purpose in action.

- Moral journalism. In exploring purpose, a fully developed ethics program might encompass "foundational ethics" for practitioners, "transformational ethics" for the profession, and "moral journalism" as an overall system—not *moralizing*, but reflecting on journalism's obligation to help citizens pay attention to the threats and opportunities that directly affect well-being and social justice.

- Journalism and democracy studies. We routinely assert that journalism is a bedrock of democratic self-rule, but we do not incorporate democratic theory into our courses or articulate our notions of democracy (beyond endorsing the First Amendment). What if we did? How might that strengthen not only the intellectual repertoire of students and practitioners but also the usefulness of practice?

- Open vs. closed cultures in news enterprises. The Readership Institute at Northwestern University has documented that the vast majority of newspapers suffer from closed cultures, shut off from learning from their environment and from other disciplines and fields. How might journalism education help open up newsroom cultures so news organizations can adapt and innovate?

The thinking journalist

Tim Porter, once a *San Francisco Examiner* senior editor, now explores the profession through his blog, First Draft. In a September 2003 post, he writes about his nine months as a blogger:

> I have read more studies about the nature of journalism and the habits of readership, more debate about what should be done to arrest the continued decline of newspapers as a mass medium, more criticism about the obdurate refusal of the industry to act

on matters it knows must be addressed as a matter of survival, and more news stories, magazine pieces, and commentary about newspapers' successes, failures, and business habits than I ever did in the 24 years I worked for newspapers.

I practiced journalism, but I knew almost nothing about it—although I thought I did. Hindsight, of course, clarifies and age, if we allow it, deepens perspective. Still, while working in a role dedicated to informing the public, I had precious little information about my own profession, about its best practitioners (or greatest charlatans), about its history and role in the development and preservation of democracy, about its standards or even about the people I intended to inform—the community around me.

A commitment to critical thinking can be the cornerstone of a distinctive identity for journalism schools. There is a great need for this. Betty Medsger, a reporter-turned-journalism educator, refers to journalists as "thinkers without thoughts"—people with "significant intellectual powers" who "have spent so much time on automatic pilot that their powers of reflection have been impaired." Phil Meyer, another journalist-scholar, notes that the profession's focus on craft is no longer adequate in a world of social, technological, and economic turbulence:

A craft is learned by emulation: watching a master perform and then imitating that person. A profession is learned from first principles so that when things change, the professional understands the changes and adjusts techniques to it. . . . Today we have a desperate need for theory, for new ways of understanding the media environment and the choices we are forced to make.

Practitioners need workable ideas, models, and data that can guide professional judgment. Journalism schools can connect practitioners to conceptual tools through conferences, consultancies, and reports aimed at newsrooms. Thus today's Tim Porters can acquire advanced research skills, the chance to publish in academic venues, and keen insights to share with other practitioners.

Transforming the field: public knowledge and public judgment

This could be the most significant domain in which journalism education engages other disciplines—and the greatest value it can produce on behalf of journalism as a discipline. Business schools are essentially schools of decision making. Journalism schools might become schools of public judgment—if they work through issues of knowledge and inquiry. Science and other observing professions constantly test and rethink their notions of what constitutes legitimate knowledge and inquiry. Scientists present their findings as uncertain, subject to revision as more is learned. In contrast, by presenting facts as complete, narratives as closed, and journalistic voice as authoritative, journalism has adopted a false posture of certainty. Anthony Smith, president of Oxford's Magdalen College, says journalism is undergoing an unconscious crisis because it "has not worked its way through the new issues and problems of knowledge."

> There are 10 ways to describe a fire, 20 reasons for an industrial conflict, 30 versions of the reasons why a set of disarmament talks breaks down, countless "causes" of a kidnapping—all the explanations being equally compelling if one adopts a different time frame or asks a different question or looks toward a different range of consequences. That has always been the case, but in the past the available explanations have been narrower. Today we have access to many more of the possible simultaneous reasons for events. The computers are full of data, all equally available, all ascertainably "true." Journalism has not failed in the sense of being unable to grapple with these or being unaware of them, but in failing to talk to readers, listeners, and viewers as if the world were compounded of uncertainties.

Journalists speak "as if the speaker of news could have no doubt ... in every story there is a fixed point of certainty, as if the reporter were *telling not enquiring*" (my emphasis), Smith writes. Journalism sees itself as a fount of information, not as a means of inquiry. Because it atomizes facts and treats each story as a separate, dated entity, journalism also fails to see itself as "a grand text . . . reflecting and feeding the *mores* of a society."

"A story about an injustice entails a narrative of justice," Smith writes. "A story of murder is based upon a narrative of the sanctity of life. Stories about corruption are implicitly about honesty, and about the prevalence of dishonesty—they are not just tellings of stories about single events." Furthermore, media logic and political logic—the foundational propositions about what each domain must do to thrive—are out of kilter. Following the media's fixation with the present, politics now favors test-marketing policy options with media-savvy citizens over taking time to build consensus in the public as a whole.

Schools can investigate the domains of public knowledge, public inquiry, public epistemology, and public heuristics—and develop new journalistic practices that explain more fully what is really happening in the world, and especially within politics. They can help journalists assess how they capture and convey public opinion—and the subsequent impact on political process. A journalism school also can help assess journalistic practices against what citizens need in order to come to public judgment.

My abiding intellectual interests concern the ways people work together to create meaning and forge connections. I am interested in the relationship of communication theory and practice to democratic theory and practice. I have been thinking and writing about fundamental questions about how citizens, communities, and institutions:

- identify what matters and what requires their attention and response,

- generate the knowledge they need to act together on public matters,

• reach public judgment and translate that judgment into action.

I think of journalism as a system of democratic inquiry—the constant effort to generate public knowledge through the exchange and testing of ideas and information among citizens. I use *citizen* here not in the *Associated Press Stylebook* definition as the "bearer of certain rights" but as "a political actor who shapes democratic life."

I have been developing a simple argument:

• Citizens are at the center of democratic self-rule;

• in a democracy, professions, crafts, institutions, associations, and officials act as agents of citizens or serve to increase the direct agency of citizens;

• therefore journalism—as a profession, craft, and/or institution— derives its authority from acting as an agent of citizens or increasing the agency of citizens.

Journalists should reflect on how our practices serve or undermine citizen agency and should experiment with practices better adapted to the continuously changing world we cover and work within. I suspect that much of the current alienation of citizens from journalism springs from practices that do not support citizens as political actors. In my experience, journalists can be hindered in serving citizens well by two forces: the market fixation of some companies that house newsrooms, and the professionalized orientation of the newsrooms themselves. Market discipline and professional discipline have important roles to play in news organizations, but neither should trump democratic discipline. Therein lies the struggle of contemporary journalism.

My professional career has had three distinct, if overlapping, phases. In the first, I worked on mastering the craft disciplines of reporting, writing, editing, and packaging news. In the second, I learned about managing and leading newsrooms, including developing systems for recruiting and diversifying newsroom staff, integrating verbal and visual journalism, understanding readers as consumers, and creating coherent and effective publications. In the third phase, I have focused on mastering strategic innovation and executive leadership.

In all three phases, I have tried to use reflection to inform practice and practice to inform reflection. Over time, I have tested three premises in news coverage, news judgment, and newsroom organization:

- <u>In a democracy, citizens are experts in their own lives and in their common aspirations</u>. Professionals, including journalists, should treat citizens as full political actors, not as passive political consumers. The perspectives and experiences of all people affected by public action must be brought to bear to reach sound public judgment about such action.

- <u>In organizations, people are experts in their own work and aspire to make meaningful and important contributions</u>. Organizations that serve democracy and community can learn much by emulating both in their internal operations. That doesn't mean voting on all decisions. It means treating each other with due regard and being explicit about who makes which decisions by which means. And it means that each of us who work in newsrooms, classrooms, and boardrooms must take responsibility for our own work and for our contributions to the whole.

- <u>In democratic communities and in organizations, the function of leadership is not to influence people to embrace the leader's vision, but to influence others to confront their own challenges, problems, and opportunities</u>. Times of transformational change can seem overwhelming—our only option is to respond as effectively as we can.

The university and public knowledge

The work of a research university is complex and challenging, onerous and honorable. A university creates, tests, conserves, and disseminates knowledge. It blends the hopes and dreams of students with the energy and insights of faculty and staff. It lures luminaries to campus to refresh the knowledge keepers and to be refreshed by them. It serves communities, professions, agencies, enterprises, and democracy overall. It responds to pressing practical needs, and it builds society's long-term capacity to adapt.

The university now grapples with two conceptions of knowledge that complicate this work. The first is the notion that knowledge is infinitely expandable by being infinitely reducible—that deconstructing all knowledge into its tiniest parts is the best way to understand the whole. Expertise increasingly consists of mastering ever-smaller increments. Discovery derives as much from parsing the known universe as imagining the unknown one. Among the consequences of this intradisciplinarity are faculties that share office space but not conceptual space. Scholars within a department may offer more to colleagues across the web than to colleagues across the hall.

The second notion is that knowledge, at its essence, is a private good. It benefits individual students and individual corporations, who therefore must bear the brunt of its cost. Knowledge as a public good is realized as the aggregation of private goods: communities with greater numbers of knowledge workers, or more patents, or other intellectual property rights, will outperform communities with fewer numbers, patents, and rights. As a consequence of privatization, universities have adopted management norms that prefer measurable cash-value contributions to the world's treasury of ideas. Meanwhile, public provenance for higher education shrinks as needs swell.

What is to be done? This is where the university can tap "the genius of the AND" as opposed to "the tyranny of the OR." A university can call upon its ability to learn from both verities and heresies, to be at once flexible and steadfast, to pursue simultaneously the practical and the ideal. A school of journalism, for example, can teach and study specific disciplines of inquiry while demonstrating the interdisciplinary collaboration inherent in creating and distributing news and other mass-media messages. And it can invoke the corporate returns from investing in professional education even as it makes a case for the public value of public knowledge. It can marry private management interests with public ends.

Journalism and mass communication give form and substance to the search for meaning and belonging. They are, in a sense, disciplines of social epistemology: They reflect collective efforts to know what is happening and to get at the meaning of things. They require the integration of knowledge and the synthesis of ideas. They are also disciplines of social and cultural studies: They shape—and are shaped by—the social fabric and cultural dynamics of our times. Mastering these dynamics can help the university capture resources to sustain the search for meaning and connection.

Those of us who love journalism and journalism education must find the right balance between what must be enduring—our purpose and values—and what must be dynamic—our practices and skills. We can renew the great traditions of print and broadcast journalism and advertising even as we lay the foundations for new media, convergent newsrooms, and new methodologies of inquiry. We can rejoice in teaching creativity as well as craft, innovation as well as tradition, invention as well as emulation.

IF NOT NOW, WHEN?

*Cole had begun a book, which would bring together
in one place much of his thinking about the ideal
roles of journalism and the public in a democratic society.
He had completed only the introduction and part
of the first chapter. That fragment is presented here,
edited for clarity.*

Introduction

We pride ourselves upon being realistic,
desiring a hardheaded cognizance of facts, and devoted
to mastering the means of life. We pride ourselves
upon a practical idealism, a lively and easily moved
faith in possibilities as yet unrealized,
in willingness to make a sacrifice for their realization.
Idealism easily becomes a sanction of waste
and carelessness, and realism a sanction of
legal formalism in behalf of things as they are—
the rights of the possessor.

John Dewey
"The Need for a Recovery of Philosophy" (1917)

I am one of those who believe that the real will never find
an irremovable basis till it rests upon the ideal.

James Russell Lowell
Democracy, and Other Addresses (1887)

SOMETIME AFTER 2 A.M. on Monday, June 22, 1964, Claude Sitton got a telephone call in his motel room in Jackson, Mississippi. He was among the first people Mary King of the Student Nonviolent Coordinating Committee (SNCC) roused from sleep to put on alert. Three SNCC workers—James Chaney, Andy Goodman, and Mickey Schwerner—were missing outside Meridian, a town whose cluster of black-owned businesses was supposed to be "a rare and wispy beacon of progress for all of Negro Mississippi."[1]

By that afternoon, Sitton was in Meridian, asking questions about the missing civil rights workers. In the rotunda of the county courthouse, just outside the sheriff's office, an angry crowd accosted Sitton and told him to get out of town. An insurance executive threatened him with bodily harm. Sitton and a colleague, Karl Fleming, sought refuge across the street at the Turner Furniture Store, run by the family of Sitton's boss back in New York City. Sitton pleaded with his boss's uncle to intercede with the crowd, to explain that Sitton was a Southerner, too, just doing his job.

"I'll tell you what," the uncle said. "If that mob gets you and Mr. Fleming down in the street and is kicking the hell out of you, I wouldn't participate in that. On the other hand, I wouldn't lift one damn finger to help you."[2]

Sitton, who grew up in Georgia, was a reporter for the *New York Times*. Doing his job had put him outside the protective kinship network often obliged by his fellow Southerners. Doing his job meant staying put in Meridian and covering what became the story of the abduction and murders of Chaney, Goodman, and Schwerner.

For years, Claude Sitton crisscrossed the South covering the Civil Rights Movement. His reporting gave solace to those who, moved by faith in unrealized possibilities, submitted to manacles, fire hoses, and German shepherds. It enraged "realists" insistent on keeping things as they were. It pressured the president to act. And it offered to all who read his dispatches a means for hardheaded cognizance of the facts.

Sitton's work on the front lines undoubtedly saved lives, as civil rights activists besieged in country churches learned that a call to him would lead to a call to their oppressors (often in law enforcement), who might think twice about maiming or killing them because the *New York Times* was on the story. He was courageous, and he was clever. He invented the now-ubiquitous reporter's notebook by cutting a stenographer's pad down so that it would fit—inconspicuously—inside his coat jacket. His civil rights coverage was the foundation of a distinguished career, as a reporter and national editor for the *Times* and then as editor-in-chief and Pulitzer Prize-winning columnist of the *News and Observer* in Raleigh, North Carolina.

Claude Sitton was my first newspaper boss. Over nearly five years at the *N&O*, I worked as obituary clerk, summer intern, City Hall reporter, religion/arts/architecture/historic-preservation reporter, and assistant city editor. I was too low in the pecking order to work directly under Claude, but the newsroom was imbued with the qualities he demanded of journalists—exactness, fairness, tenacity, the swift pursuit of the news, and an itch for justice. I learned the discipline of my craft in Claude Sitton's newsroom.

I began paying attention to journalism when I began paying attention to the world. I had just graduated from high school when the *New York Times* stood firm against the Nixon administration and published the secret history of the Vietnam War known as the Pentagon Papers. I was a sophomore in college when the *Washington Post* began peeling back the layers of political skullduggery and constitutional recklessness that became known as Watergate. In my senior year, I became editor of the *Daily Tar Heel*, thrilled to join such illustrious predecessors as novelist Thomas Wolfe, polling pioneer Lou Harris, and journalists Charles Kuralt, Edwin Yoder, and Jonathan Yardley.

In the 25 years since, I have worked as a reporter, assistant city editor, metro editor, assistant managing editor, managing editor, and editor-in-chief. I edited a magazine and helped guide the transition of two newspapers into the convergent world in which a single reporter's work can be distributed on paper, online, and on television.

I have worked alongside journalists who had won, or would win, our craft's highest honors—prizes named for Joseph Pulitzer, Ernie Pyle, and other pillars of the profession. I have sat in judgment of journalists' best work, as a Pulitzer Prize juror and a judge for the National Press Photographers' Pictures of the Year awards and a host of state press contests. I have seen the continuous improvement of newspapering's crafts—reporting, writing, photography, graphics, design, editorial cartooning, criticism, and commentary. I have learned an incredible amount from my colleagues—and have seen how journalism, well done and well directed, can advance the public good.

And yet, I also have watched journalists become increasingly dispirited about their work and news companies become flummoxed about their futures. Worse yet, I have witnessed citizens becoming increasingly alienated from the journalists who strive to serve them. In addition to being dissatisfied with the way the news media portray our lives and our world, the evidence shows, we also are dissatisfied with the way politics—our public life—works. The two kinds of dissatisfaction are related in profoundly important ways.

This book, therefore, is a study of politics and journalism. Both fields drive, and express, the ways we collectively make sense of the world, make tough choices and exert energy in the conduct and improvement of our public life. This book contemplates how we can attend to what truly matters. It seeks a path among the light and shade of realism and idealism, a path illuminated by both notions but overshadowed by neither.

Why might citizens, scholars, and professionals who are not journalists read a book about what ails journalism and what might heal it? Journalism plays a central role in determining how public life works and who feels included in, or excluded from, it. Much of what we learn about public life and journalism can cast light on the relationship between public life and other fields of work and thought. And journalism is immediately accessible for study—as near at hand as a newspaper, magazine, radio dial, television remote, or computer keyboard.

I have situated myself in the tradition of journalism—calling out the names of some of those who have inspired and taught me, cataloguing the kinds of jobs I've had— to avow that I am a part of this tradition. But I also find myself outside it. I have studied journalism from the perspectives of citizens, scholars, and professionals, because I am a member of these groups, too, and because looking at one's lifework from a variety of vantage points is highly educating. This book is informed by my being both a part of, and apart from, journalism's tradition.

As a public journalist, I feel obliged to make explicit the motivations and moral underpinnings of this work. The rest of this introduction considers purpose, what it means to me to work as a journalist, a professional, a scholar, and a citizen. The four sections that follow are framed as ways to act publicly—to make public life go well, to repair the world, to act in concert, and to be accountable. They are also "Etch-a-Sketch®" essays" on the state of the world and the plan and purposes of the book, beginning with the first of several elaborations of the term *public journalism*.

To help public life go well: public journalism

Public journalism is at once a movement that has been around for more than a decade and an emerging set of journalistic practices. At its essence, public journalism aspires to reconnect people, public life, and the press in a more potent combination for the use of *citizens as political actors*. There are any number of ways this might be done, and public journalists have spent more than a decade studying democratic theory and practice and experimenting with journalistic practice (and theory). Some have asked candidates running for office to discuss issues named as important by citizens. Some have convened town hall meetings or community conversations of citizens. The unifying commitment is treating citizens as political actors, not just as news consumers, political spectators, or a mass audience. Public journalism examines who acts in democracy, what they act on, when and where they act, why they act, and how they act—applying the five *W*'s and an *H* of journalistic inquiry to citizens. And it examines what impedes citizens in acting effectively as political actors—including journalistic practices.

The quickest way to determine whether a journalist is doing public journalism is to engage her in a discussion of the role of citizens. Traditional practitioners see their work as giving readers, listeners, viewers, and browsers—the *who*—information and "letting them decide." They are less clear about how the other *W*'s and the *H* apply to citizens: what do citizens decide, when, where, why, and how? The principal journalistic rule book in the United States, the *Associated Press Stylebook and Briefing on Media Law*, discourages journalists from using the word *citizen* in stories unless referring to a person's legal standing as the member of a nation. ("To avoid confusion, use *resident*, not *citizen*, in referring to inhabitants of states and cities.")[3] Traditional practitioners tend to think of the people who rely on journalism as consumers, as audience members and, in political contexts, as voters. Voting is one form of political action, but only one. Voter—albeit a step up from inhabitant or resident—is a narrowly prescribed political role.

Public journalism has attracted considerable attention and controversy, both by critiquing traditional practice and by experimenting with new practices.[4] Many establishment practitioners decry public journalism as pandering to common people, or kowtowing to corporate bosses, or puckering up to philanthropic foundations that have underwritten some of the exploration and experimentation. Other practitioners, while still disavowing public journalism, now use some of its techniques or concepts. More strident critics of the press, such as Thomas Frank of the *Baffler*, dismiss public journalism as perhaps well-intentioned but misguided (and middlebrow) in embracing "the majesty of The People," "soft populism," and "the market as an inherently democratic arrangement" instead of assaulting the institutional power of conglomerate press ownership.[5]

Astute scholarly critics, such as Theodore Glasser of Stanford University, Michael Schudson of the University of California at San Diego, and John Pauly of St. Louis University, have advanced public journalism by taking it seriously even as they take it apart critically. Glasser, like Frank, worries that public journalism lacks "a theory of the good" or of justice, disregards "the realities of political power," and could give citizens a false sense of participation without challenging elite interests. Schudson says public journalism confuses "community" with "society" with "public discourse," each of which entails different dynamics. Pauly says public journalism lacks a sophisticated grasp of culture.[6] These are all legitimate challenges, which will be addressed in this book.

Even the term *public journalism* has drawn fire. "What, for instance, is the rest of journalism supposed to be called—non-public journalism? Private journalism?" asks Barbie Zelizer of the University of Pennsylvania.[7] (Public journalism has been called by other names as well, most significantly "civic journalism."[8]) The word *public* has many meanings in the American vernacular. Public journalism uses it the way Jay Rosen of New York University suggests when he writes:

> A public is something more than a market for information, an audience for spectacle, or a pollster's random sample. Publics are formed when we turn from our private and separate affairs to face common problems, and to face each other in dialogue and discussion. . . . "The public," in whose name all journalists ply their trade, is best understood as an achievement of good journalism—its intended outcome rather than its assumed audience.[9]

Public journalism invites citizens into public relationships.

Rosen, a journalism professor, brought to public journalism much of its conceptual foundation through a series of articles, monographs, and workshops run by the Project on Public Life and the Press, which he directed for five years. The best historical summary of public journalism is his book *What Are Journalists For?*[10] The book before you stands on the shoulders of Rosen, Davis "Buzz" Merritt, Lisa Austin, Art Charity, and others who have assayed public journalism. This book pulls together accounts of politics, public life, and journalistic practice into a more complete statement of what public journalism can be when fully realized. Public journalists have engaged citizens directly in thinking about political issues or campaigns but not so much in thinking through public journalism itself. Therefore this book is aimed at citizens as first among equals, to bring you into the conversation—alongside scholars and professionals, journalists in particular.

"When politics goes well, we can know a good in common that we cannot know alone," Michael Sandel, a political philosopher at Harvard, has said.[11] "The press can try to make public life 'go well' in Sandel's sense, and hope for a restoration of its authority, some relief from the grim spiral of cynicism and mistrust," Jay Rosen has said. "Journalism can do all this without departing from its central mission to inform and enlighten, without surrendering its important role as watchdog and critic, without boring us with civics lessons or hyping itself as the answer to all our ills."[12]

To repair the world: disruption and democratic anxiety

Journalists are drawn to the craft for many reasons. Some of us are fascinated by politics, or sports, or business, or religion, and fuel our fascination through news work. Some of us like to tell stories in words or images. Some of us simply like finding things out. Most journalists, if you probe, will tell you that part of what calls us to this work is a desire to make the world a better place. "Always fight for progress and reform," Joseph Pulitzer admonished his journalistic heirs in the platform that runs daily on the editorial page of the *St. Louis Post-Dispatch*. I take this section heading from the Hebrew phrase *tikkun olam*, which means "to repair (or heal, or transform) the world."[13]

The world certainly could use some repair. The 20th century, to update Charles Dickens, was the best and worst of times. Millions died in industrialized slaughter in Turkish Armenia, the Holocaust, and Stalin's reign of terror; millions more in genocidal eruptions in Southeast Asia, the Balkans, and Africa. As many as 2.5 million Germans died, many from hunger and disease, when they were expelled from postwar Poland and Czechoslovakia.[14] The partition of India and Pakistan led to about a million deaths, and another million died when Bangladesh seceded from India.[15] Weapons escalated in destructive capacity, from gas to biological weapons to the means of nuclear annihilation. Civil and human rights were brutally suppressed in the American South, Latin America, South Africa, the Soviet bloc, India, and China. "The decisions of a few people," Jonathan Glover, a medical ethicist in London, writes, "can mean horror and death for hundreds of thousands, even millions, of other people."[16] All told, 160 million people died in war and systemic violence, and we still face "the risk that whole nations will be destroyed."[17]

During the same century, however, ordinary people seized the opportunity to do great things together. Peter Ackerman and Jack Duvall, authors and documentary producers, cite nonviolent people's movements in Russia, India, Denmark, El Salvador, the American South, Poland, Argentina, Chile, the Philippines, the West Bank and Gaza, South Africa, Czechoslovakia and across Eastern Europe, and Burma, among others. "Tyrants were toppled, governments were overthrown, occupying armies were impeded, and political systems that withheld human rights were shattered," Ackerman and Duvall write. "Entire societies were transformed, suddenly or gradually, by people using nonviolent resistance to destroy their opponents' ability to steer events."[18] Meanwhile, we have achieved substantial gains in life expectancy, literacy, industrial and agricultural productivity, and per-capita income around the world, including in developing countries.[19]

Now we are buffeted by accelerating, and differential, rates of change—and with change come gain and loss, progress and decay. We experience transformational change in all aspects of our lives—at work, home, and play; within families and neighborhoods; among peoples and nations. The changes are economic, political, social, technological, physical. The very basis of our individual and collective being—our genes—are being manipulated, presaging a break in what it means to be human. We are at risk of overtaxing the Earth's capacity to sustain human life and industrialized production. Given the assault of AIDS, Ebola virus, mad-cow and foot-and-mouth disease, we fear that new viral/bacterial/fungal plagues will elude modern medicine and blight our food or our bodies. We are widening the gap between rich and poor—within the workplace, within the United States, and between developed and developing countries. Ethnic and racial animosities abound as genocide stalks its prey beneath the decrepit sheepskin of "ethnic cleansing."[20]

Zygmunt Bauman, an emeritus professor of sociology at the Universities of Leeds and Warsaw, argues that we are in a cauldron of *unsicherheit*. He uses the German word because it carries three meanings, which no single English word conveys: lack of security (in achievements, standards, habits, and skills), lack of certainty (about how we might understand the world), and lack of safety (in our persons, property, home, and "home ground.")[21]

> The absence or dearth of any of the three ingredients [security, certainty, safety] has much the same effect: the dissipation of self-assurance, the loss of trust in one's own ability and the other people's intentions, growing incapacitation, anxiety, cageyness, the tendency to fault-seeking and fault-finding, to scapegoating and aggression. All such tendencies are symptoms of *gnawing existential mistrust* . . . anxiety is unspecific, and the resulting fear may be easily blamed on wrong causes and may prompt actions glaringly irrelevant to the genuine cause; genuine reasons for agitation being difficult to locate and even less

easy to control if discovered, there is a powerful temptation to construe and name putative, yet credible culprits against whom one can wage a sensible defensive (or, better still, offensive) action.[22]

Bauman cites economic globalization outstripping political institutions' capacity to respond:

> Power is increasingly removed from politics, a circumstance which accounts simultaneously for growing political apathy, the progressive disinterestedness of the electorate in everything 'political' except the juicy scandals perpetrated by top people in the limelight, and the waning of expectations that salvation may come from government buildings, whoever their current or future occupants may be.[23]

Not surprisingly, democracy's apparent high tide around the globe is accompanied by a serious undertow. "While very few dare to openly challenge the liberal-democratic model, the signs of disaffection with present institutions are becoming widespread," writes Chantal Mouffe of the Centre for the Study of Democracy at the University of Westminster in Great Britain:

> An increasing number of people feel that traditional parties have ceased to take their interests into account, and extreme right-wing parties are making important inroads in many European countries. Moreover, even among those who are resisting the call of the demagogues, there is a marked cynicism about politics and politicians, and this has a very corrosive effect on popular adhesion to democratic values. There is clearly a negative force at work in most liberal-democratic societies, which contradicts the triumphalism that we have witnessed since the collapse of Soviet communism.[24]

What emerges is a political system that cannot address the causes of anxiety but can deflect it onto political scapegoats. Democratic means can be used for undemocratic ends. Jewelle Taylor Gibbs and Teiahsha Bankhead, scholars of social policy at the University of California at Berkeley, argue that a series of voter initiatives passed in California in the late 1990s—increasing penalties on criminals, stripping illegal immigrants of eligibility for social services, abandoning affirmative action, and eliminating bilingual education—were prompted by projections that California would have a nonwhite majority in the first decade of the 21st century. The propositions were advanced by those who wanted to slow the increase in people of color or at least "limit their socio-economic mobility and weaken their potential political power."[25] David Broder of the *Washington Post* describes the initiative process as "democracy derailed" because moneyed interests can circumvent duly elected representative bodies and enact legislative programs through strategic, but not necessarily deliberative, campaigns.[26] Daniel Smith, a political scientist at the University of Denver, reaches similar conclusions about the "*faux populism*" behind anti-tax ballot initiatives.[27]

And so we find ourselves at a point of seeming paradox. Democracy is ascendant around the globe. Technology and the marketplace are giving affluent consumers an amazing proliferation of choices. Advances in science are generating mounds of new knowledge about how the world works and might be made to work differently. And yet alienation from government and politics grows, our abundant choices seem trivial or meaningless, and accumulating knowledge threatens to distract or overwhelm us more than to enlighten us even as scientific discovery is poised to transform our very being.

The disjunction between citizens and public life is not a new discovery. In 1959, sociologist C. Wright Mills raised the same kind of alarms:

> Nowadays men often feel that their private lives are a series
> of traps. They sense that within their everyday worlds, they
> cannot overcome their troubles, and in this feeling they are
> often quite correct: What ordinary men are directly aware

of and what they try to do are bounded by the private orbits in which they live; their visions and their powers are limited to the close-up scenes of job, family, neighborhood; in other milieux, they move vicariously and remain spectators. And the more aware they become, however vaguely, of ambitions and of threats which transcend their immediate locales, the more trapped they seem to feel. . . . They do not possess the quality of mind essential to grasp the interplay of man and society, of biography and history, of self and world. They cannot cope with their personal troubles in such ways as to control the structural transformations that usually lie behind them.[28]

Mills attributes the missing "quality of mind" not to limited human capacity, but to social scientists and "literary men" failing to help people develop the skills to connect self and world. Forty years later, Russell Jacoby, a historian at the University of California, Los Angeles, echoes Mills:

We have entered the era of acquiescence, in which we build our lives, families and careers with little expectation the future [political prospects] will diverge from the present. . . . A new consensus has emerged: There are no alternatives. This is the wisdom of our times, an age of political exhaustion and retreat.[29]

Worldwide upheaval, disruptive technology, the loss of security-certainty-safety, the globalization Godzilla, politics stripped of power, democratic disaffection, life as a series of traps, acquiescent exhaustion, and retreat: 40-plus years of political alienation seems an undue handicap. Old systems, old frameworks need repair or replacement.

To act in concert: the book as conversation—and argument

This book argues that public life is not going as well at it could—and must do better if we are to respond effectively to the anxieties and disruptions that continually confront us. The argument draws upon shared experience, science and social science, and philosophy. By *argument*, I do not refer to shouting matches or general disagreeability, although both can be part of fierce contests. I mean argument as a tool of cooperation as well as of conflict. To borrow from (and corrupt a bit) the German philosopher Immanuel Kant (1724-1804), a good argument requires thinking for oneself, thinking in the place of others, and thinking out loud together. A good argument sharpens everyone's thinking.

This book is also imagined as an inclusive conversation—among citizens, scholars, and professionals. No one group knows enough or touches enough to salvage politics or revitalize public life by itself. Anthony O'Hear, director of the Royal Institute of Philosophy in Britain, suggests some scholarly conversants:

> It is the thought of Plato and Aristotle, of St. Augustine and other thinkers of the Christian tradition, of Bacon and Newton, of Diderot and Voltaire, of Rousseau and Kant, of Burke and Herder, of de Tocqueville and Nietzsche, of Marx, Darwin, and Freud, and of their critics and opponents that has made us what we are. If we want to understand our present state, we have to confront the ideas of these and other thinkers of the remote or recent past, and take a stand on them, one way or another. Otherwise we will be simply fumbling in the thickets of the present, unable to see the wood for the trees.[30]

Many of these thinkers—and women and non-Europeans often neglected in stringing together such strands—will be drawn into this conversation. Among them are Hannah Arendt, Jane Addams, and Mary Parker Follett, 20th-century activists and thinkers. The conversation also will call upon American pragmatists, including William James, John Dewey, and Richard Rorty, and political and social theorists, such as Benjamin Barber, Jürgen Habermas, Mona Harrington, Ann Oakley, and Cornel West.

A book isn't really a conversation, but I have tried to imbue this one with a conversational spirit and to keep the conversation open to anyone unfamiliar with some terms or participants. I quote people at length so we can hear their voices as well as their ideas. I identify major contributors—even Plato and Kant—by discipline and, if dead, by nationality and life span. I use personal pronouns inclusively—*I* for my own voice and experience; *you* to address you, the reader; *we* as subjects of the discussion in lieu of "people" as objects of it. *We* may refer to members of one group—*we citizens* or *we journalists*—and I try to make those usages clear. (If *we* excludes you or frustrates you by its overuse, I ask your forbearance.) I mix up *he* and *she* and use *one* sparingly in generalizations. (Some conversants use *man* generically; I don't mess with their words.) I avoid *they* as much as possible, because it is too easy to fob off responsibility on *them*.

A conversation requires a common tongue, and that is a challenge. Journalists are particular about their words (and images), while scholars are obsessive about theirs. So I have worked to write in a supple idiom, with occasional inflections favored by one group more than another. For citizens, I have tried to write in a language that respects intelligence and a desire to be included in, not mystified out of, the conversation. For scholars and professionals outside journalism, I have tried to use language that respects precision and erudition—and to offer extensive footnotes and bibliography (even though these may be distracting for more casual readers). For journalists, I have tried to write in a language that respects clarity and that aspires, on occasion, to grace.[31]

The genius of the English language is its elasticity, but some foundational terms for this conversation—*politics*, *public*, *citizen*, among others—have been stretched like five-year-old waistbands: they can barely hold up any specific meaning. I hope we can refurbish them together. *Politics* in particular is a bruised word, and most of us recoil from it the way we pull back from a blackened banana. We associate it with the schmoozing and backstabbing of office politics, with the anesthetized imagination of politics-as-usual, with the sleazy self-gratification of politics as pornography.

"All human action lies under the shadow of prospective regret," writes John Dunn, a political theorist at the University of Cambridge. "But there are few, if any, domains of our acting over which that shadow falls so darkly as it does over the huge, and ever more dramatically consequential, field of politics."[32]

In the chapters that follow, this book strives to lift that shadow a bit by developing the following argument:

We create the world we inhabit through the institutions we make and actions we take. We form this world through our words and deeds; at a minimum, we support it through our acquiescence.[33] Our political, economic, civic, and social arrangements reflect the way we conceive of human beings—our philosophy of the human condition. Our actions are often guided by tacit and implicit theories, models, and metaphors about how this world works. We should make our philosophies and theories as unquiet and explicit as possible so we can examine, debate, and, as needed, amend or abandon them and the arrangements and actions predicated upon them. Unexamined idealism can become careless; unexamined realism can become repressive.

We inhabit the world we create with everyone else—so it must be a shareable world. All humans are the same and different, which prompts biologist Paul Ehrlich of Stanford University to promote the phrase *human natures*: "The universals that bind people together at any point in our evolution are covered in the word *human*. The word *natures* emphasizes the differences that gives us our individuality, our cultural variety, and our potential for future genetic and—especially—cultural evolution."[34] Because we are so much the same and so different, our coexistence is a combination of *coordination*, *cooperation*, and *conflict* (often expressed as *competition*). We coordinate so that we can each pursue our own ends with minimal interference from one another.[35] We cooperate because we are similar, sharing an immediate bond of familiarity, and because we are different, valuing what the other party brings to an endeavor. We compete because we are different, valuing our own contributions to an endeavor more than the alternatives, and because we are similar, hoping to distinguish ourselves from others like us.

Our arrangements to mediate coordination, cooperation, and conflict/competition are the means by which we create a *shareable world*—a world in which we can coexist alongside others who are like us or different from us. I use the phrase pointedly: given the unending diversity of human experience, it is easier to conceive—and more tolerable to inhabit—a shareable world than a common or universal world.[36]

Creating a shareable world involves continuous choice, not control. Given the human variety, nothing can be predetermined. The world is far too complex for an individual or institution to control our shared destiny. Control is unattainable; therefore choice is unavoidable. We will never arrive at a set point where we can stop attending to coordination, cooperation, and conflict. We must constantly adapt in the pursuit of what a biologist would call equilibrium and a Founding Father would call happiness or domestic tranquility.

Choice work requires participation in politics and public life. Making good choices requires levels of knowledge and commitment that can be generated only by the active participation of the widest array of people who are affected by the choices. Certain tasks can be delegated to politicians and parties, officeholders and offices, scholars and professionals. But politics in its essential meaning—to participate in the *polis*, the shared community—cannot be handed off to someone else. It is the inescapable work of citizens. And only by partaking in politics can each of us realize fully who we are.

Rabbi Hillel, one of the most revered scholars in Jewish history, asked: "If I am not for myself, who is for me? If I care only for myself, what am I? If not now, when?" These questions inform this book's search for ways we can reengage as citizens with the theory and practice of politics and public life.

Calling people to politics and public life is the essential purpose of journalism. Journalism cannot do politics for us. No one can. But journalism can equip us, encourage us, sustain us, and console us as we wrestle with the opportunities, challenges, fortunes, and misfortunes of the world we share.

In the United States, the world of politics has been created and re-created by fierce debates over contested truths as citizens and non-citizens have grappled over power by recasting the meaning of such terms as *utility, natural rights, the people, government, the state, interests*, and *freedom*. In this sense, talk *is* action. "We *do* things with words; William James was never more profoundly right than in that assertion," writes historian Daniel Rodgers of Princeton University. "Out of them we fashion arguments; we persuade, maneuver for space and advantage. Political words take their meaning from the tasks to which their users bend them. . . . Words are tools, often weapons; the vocabulary of politics is contested terrain and always has been."[37]

Journalism can do more to help citizens, scholars, and professionals engage in the continuing contests over truths, ideas, words, and actions—and in the work of helping communities succeed. Davis "Buzz" Merritt, the long-time editor of the *Wichita Eagle* in Kansas, defines a successful community as one whose members know what is going on and take responsibility for it.[38] I am inspired by that pragmatic definition and struggle with how best to translate it into journalistic practice. Now I appreciate it in two dimensions. The first is knowing what is happening and taking responsibility for it in the concrete world of experience. The second is knowing what is happening in our own minds—in constructing mental models, developing and applying theory, contesting the political meaning of words—and taking responsibility for that, too. What *works*, in theory and practice, is the argument and the conversation I hope this book advances.

To be accountable: purpose, craft, use

"A person's work gives her purposes a body: a shape, a history of projects and products that carry them from the mind into the world," says Jedediah Purdy, a wise young West Virginian, book-jacket proud of his home-schooling and studies at Phillips Exeter, Harvard, and Yale. "We know that this is where we are tested, where the seriousness of our purposes and the adequacy of our knowledge are up for general estimation." He continues:

> A marriage of commitment and knowledge produces dignified work. I think of this achievement through the idea of the craftsman, perhaps because I have known craftsmen well and admired their work, perhaps because the solidity of their labor ties ideas to sound and reliable things. His enduring quality of dignity arises from the fact that his work is luminous to him, in its process and its purpose. He understands the application of every tool he uses; many of them he may be able to make or repair himself. He can judge the quality of his materials because he understands what they must contribute to his product and just how that contribution will be made. Because he understands the use of his product as well, he knows just what it is to make it well or badly.[39]

Purdy describes the essence of pragmatic liberalism—solidly tying *ideas* to "sound and reliable things," or *practice*.[40] Pragmatic scholars and professionals move between ideas encapsulated in theory and practice expressed in work, hoping to use each to enrich the other. Purdy notes that a craftsperson judges her work in three dimensions—*purpose, craft*, or process (tools, materials, and how she applies both), and *use*, which determines "just what it is to make it well or badly."

I want to be held accountable for how well I have served purpose, craft, and use. My purpose is to reclaim (or recast) some key terms, such as *public*, and offer new theories and practices, or syntheses of theories and practices, in order to strengthen democracy and journalism. My craft can be assessed by the thoroughness of my research, transparency of my thinking, and clarity of my writing. Usefulness can be tested against whether the book advances an argument that others can join, keeps open a conversation about politics and journalism, and makes accessible for such discussions an array of ideas from philosophy, political theory, and social science. Let the estimation proceed.

End Notes

[1] Taylor Branch, *Pillar of Fire: America in the King Years, 1963-65* (New York: Touchstone, 1998), 361.

[2] Branch, *Pillar of Fire*, Chapter 26, "Bogue Chito Swamp," 361-374; the uncle's comment is on 364.

[3] Norm Goldstein, ed., *The Associated Press Stylebook and Briefing on Media Law* (Cambridge, MA: Perseus Publishing, 2000), 49. The *AP Stylebook* follows *Black's Law Dictionary*, which also defines *citizen* in terms of membership in a political community, "owing allegiance and being entitled to the enjoyment of full civil rights." Unlike the *AP Stylebook*, however, *Black's Law* cites the Fourteenth Amendment to the US Constitution in stating that a citizen of the United States is also a citizen "of the state wherein they reside." *Black's Law Dictionary*, Fifth Edition (St. Paul, MN: West Publishing, 1979), 221.

[4] The universe of possible citations for this point is quite large. The work we did at the *Virginian-Pilot* attracted scholars from around the country and journalists from around the globe—and occasional guffaws from establishment journalists. ("Excuse me while I run screaming from the room," David Remnick wrote about our Public Life team in "Scoop," *New Yorker*, January 29, 1996, 42.) Here is a sampler of citations from the trade press and academic scholarship just about the *Pilot* and my tenure at the *St. Louis Post-Dispatch*: Carl Sessions Stepp, "Reinventing the Newsroom," *American Journalism Review*, April 1995, 28-33; Janet Weaver, "An American Editor: Agent of Change Moves to St. Louis," *The American Editor*, November 1996, 21-24; Alicia C. Shepard, "The Change Agents," *American Journalism Review*, May 1998, 42-49; Geneva Overholser, "Editor, Inc.," *American Journalism Review*, December 1998, 60-61; Carl Sessions Stepp, "The State of the American Newspaper: Then and Now," *American Journalism Review*, September 1999, 60-73; Brent Cunningham, "The Most Important Relationship," *Columbia Journalism Review*, May/June 2000, 32-36; James Fallows, Chapter 6, "News and Democracy," in *Breaking the News: How the Media Undermine Democracy* (New York: Pantheon, 1996), 235-269; Edmund B. Lambeth,

"Public Journalism as Cultural Change," in *Assessing Public Journalism,* eds. Edmund B. Lambeth, Philip E. Meyer, and Esther Thorson (Columbia, MO: University of Missouri Press, 1998), 232-250; Jay Rosen, *What Are Journalists For?* (New Haven, CT: Yale University Press, 1999), especially Chapter 4, "Does It Help the Citizen Decide? The Intellectual Journey of the *Virginian-Pilot,*" 128-155; Alicia C. Shepard, "The End of the Line," *American Journalism Review,* Vol. 22, No. 6, July/August 2000, 44-51.

⁵ Thomas Frank, "Triangulation Nation: Journalism in the Age of Markets," in *One Market Under God* (New York: Anchor Books, 2001), 307-340, especially 312-320.

⁶ Theodore L. Glasser, ed., *The Idea of Public Journalism* (New York: Guilford Press, 1999). See Glasser's introduction, "The Idea of Public Journalism," 3-18; Michael Schudson, "What Public Journalism Knows about Journalism but Doesn't Know about 'Public,'" 188-133, and John J. Pauly, "Journalism and the Sociology of Public Life," 134-151.

⁷ Barbie Zelizer, "Making the Neighborhood Work: The Improbabilities of Public Journalism," in Glasser, *The Idea of Public Journalism,* 162.

⁸ Civic journalism has gotten increasing play through the activities of the Pew Center for Civic Journalism, a program of the Pew Charitable Trusts, a 10-year program that runs seminars and awards grants to journalists undertaking experiments in journalism. Other names include "communitarian journalism" and "community journalism" because of the central role of community in public journalism. Public journalism does not embrace communitarianism as a political philosophy, however, and "community journalism" is generally regarded as describing the highly localized journalism in small-town or neighborhood newspapers.

⁹ Jay Rosen, "Public Journalism: First Principles," in *Public Journalism: Theory and Practice* (Dayton, Ohio: Kettering Foundation, 1994).

¹⁰ Jay Rosen, *What Are Journalists For?*

¹¹ Michael J. Sandel, *Liberalism and the Limits of Justice,* second edition (Cambridge: Cambridge University Press, 1982, 1998), 183.

¹² Jay Rosen, *Getting the Connections Right: Public Journalism and the Troubles in the Press* (New York: Twentieth Century Fund Press, 1996), 6.

¹³ Michael Lerner, *Jewish Renewal: A Path to Healing and Transformation* (New York: Grossett/Putnam, 1994), 29, 33.

¹⁴ Norman M. Naimark, *Fires of Hatred: Ethnic Cleansing in Twentieth-Century Europe* (Cambridge, MA: Harvard University Press, 2001), 14 and Chapter 4, "The Expulsion of Germans from Poland and Czechoslovakia," 108-138.

¹⁵ Russell Jacoby, *The End of Utopia: Politics and Culture in an Age of Apathy* (New York: Basic Books, 1999), 168.

¹⁶ Jonathan Glover, *Humanity: A Moral History of the Twentieth Century* (New Haven, CT: Yale University Press, 1999), 3.

[17] Robert S. McNamara and James G. Blight, *Wilson's Ghost: Reducing the Risk of Conflict, Killing and Catastrophe in the 21st Century* (New York: PublicAffairs, 2001), xv. Historian J. M. Roberts says the death toll associated with the two world wars alone, conservatively estimated, may have been 100 million lives. J. M. Roberts, *Twentieth Century: A History of the World from 1901 to 2000* (London: Allen Lane, 1999).

[18] Peter Ackerman and Jack Duvall, *A Force More Powerful: A Century of Nonviolent Conflict* (New York: St. Martin's Press, 2000), 1-9; the quotation is on 2.

[19] McNamara and Blight, *Wilson's Ghost*, xv.

[20] Any number of sources discuss these threats in considerable detail. Here are five that are well wrought and usefully provocative on particular topics: genocide, Naimark, *Fires of Hatred*; environmental destruction, J. R. McNeill, *Something New Under the Sun: An Environmental History of the Twentieth-Century World* (New York, W. W. Norton, 2000); human health and genetics, Paul R. Ehrlich, *Human Natures: Genes, Cultures, and the Human Prospect* (Washington, DC: Island Press, 2000); globalization, Michael Hardt and Antonio Negri, *Empire* (Cambridge, MA: Harvard University Press, 2000); scenarios, Allen Hammond, *Which World? Scenarios for the 21st Century* (Washington, DC: Island Press, 1998).

[21] Zygmunt Bauman, *In Search of Politics* (Stanford, CA: Stanford University Press, 1999), 17.

[22] Ibid., 17-18

[23] Ibid., 19.

[24] Chantal Mouffe, *The Democratic Paradox* (London: Verso, 2000), 80.

[25] Jewelle Taylor Gibbs and Teiahsha Bankhead, *Preserving Privilege: California Politics, Propositions and People of Color* (Westport, CT: Praeger, 2001), quotation from x. The fourth proposition, 227, on bilingual education, required a two-thirds majority to be repealed—an effective block against minority-turned-majority blocs overturning the measure once they attain a simple majority. Proposition 227 passed by less than a two-thirds majority, 61 percent to 39 percent, in June 1998 (123).

[26] David S. Broder, *Democracy Derailed: Initiative Campaigns and the Power of Money* (New York: Harcourt Inc., 2000).

[27] Daniel A. Smith, *Tax Crusaders and the Politics of Direct Democracy* (New York: Routledge, 1998).

[28] C. Wright Mills, *The Sociological Imagination* (New York: Oxford University Press, 1959, 2000), 3-4. The reference to the failings of "literary men" is on 17.

[29] Jacoby, *The End of Utopia*, xi-xii.

[30] Anthony O'Hear, *After Progress: Finding the Old Way Forward* (New York: Bloomsbury, 2001), ix-x.

[31] I follow the counsel of C. Wright Mills in his lovely essay, "On Intellectual Craftsmanship":

In many academic circles today anyone who tries to write in a widely intelligible way is liable to be condemned as a "mere literary man" or, worse still, "a mere journalist." Perhaps you have already learned that these phrases, as commonly used, only indicate the spurious inference: superficial because readable. ... To write is to raise a claim for the attention of readers. That is part of *any* style. ... Any writing—perhaps apart from that of certain truly great stylists—that is not imaginable as human speech is bad writing. ... As a member of the academic community you should think of yourself as a representative of a truly great language, and you should expect and demand of yourself that when you speak or write you try to carry on the discourse of civilized man.

From Mills, *The Sociological Imagination*, 218-222. I take clarity and grace from Joseph M. Williams, *Style: Ten Lessons in Clarity and Grace*, Fifth Edition (New York: Longman, 1997).

[32] John Dunn, *The Cunning of Unreason: Making Sense of Politics* (New York: Basic Books, 2000), x.

[33] The idea of acquiescence in this context is developed by Russell Hardin, *Liberalism, Constitutionalism, and Democracy* (Oxford: Oxford University Press, 1999).

[34] Paul R. Ehrlich, *Human Natures: Genes, Cultures, and the Human Prospect,* ix-x.

[35] Russell Hardin elaborates on coordination as an expression of mutual advantage throughout *Liberalism, Constitutionalism, and Democracy.*

[36] I take the phrase *shareable world* from Toni Morrison, the Nobel laureate in literature, who uses it to describe a world readers and writers struggle to realize together through acts of imagination. Toni Morrison, *Playing in the Dark: Whiteness and the Literary Imagination* (New York: Vintage Books, 1992), xii-xiii. Elizabeth Minnich of The Union Institute brought the phrase and its source to my attention.

[37] Daniel T. Rodgers, *Contested Truths: Keywords in American Politics Since Independence* (Cambridge, MA: Harvard University Press, 1987), 10-11.

[38] See David Mathews, *Politics for People*, Second Edition (Urbana and Chicago, IL: University of Illinois Press, 1999), 191.

[39] Jedediah Purdy, *For Common Things: Irony, Trust and Commitment in America Today* (New York: Alfred A. Knopf, 1999), 199.

[40] See Charles W. Anderson, *Pragmatic Liberalism* (Chicago: University of Chicago Press, 1990). Purdy's notion of luminous labor also encapsulates 25 years of experience with quality circles, total quality management, and customer focus. See Richard C. Whiteley, *The Customer-Driven Company: Moving from Talk to Action* (Reading, MA: Addison-Wesley, 1990), and Regis McKenna, *Real Time: Preparing for the Age of the Never Satisfied Customer* (Boston: Harvard Business School Press, 1997).

CHAPTER ONE

Everybody knows that pestilences have a way of
recurring in the world; yet somehow we find it hard
to believe in ones that crash down on our heads from
a blue sky. There have been as many plagues
as wars in history; yet always plagues and wars
take people equally by surprise.

Albert Camus
The Plague

ON A MID-SUMMER DAY in 1942, an Austrian Jew named Stekler sat alone on a bus parked alongside others in the market square of Le Chambon sur Lignon, a village in the mountains of southwest France. Stekler had been arrested by the Vichy government, collaborators with the Third Reich after the Germans overwhelmed the French on the battlefield in 1940. Now Vichy police were rounding up Jews for internment and deportation to "the East"—the Nazi death camps.

As Stekler sat in the bus, surrounded by gendarmes, 13-year-old Jean-Pierre Trocmé, the eldest son of Pastor André Trocmé, reached through the window to offer his last piece of rationed imitation chocolate. Other villagers approached to share gifts, mostly food from their depleted larders. The prisoner soon sat beside a pile nearly his own size. No matter the risk of reprisal for their public identification with this lone victim of repression, the villagers—the Chambonnais—would not turn their backs on Stekler. He was alone on the bus, but not alone in the world.[1]

"The police remained in Le Chambon for three weeks," reports Philip Hallie, chronicler of Le Chambon's resistance, "firing up their motorcycles early in the morning, trying to surprise any Jews who might have tired of life in hiding and gone back to the homes that had been sheltering them. They found no more Jews."[2]

During four years of German rule over France, Le Chambon and neighboring villages created and sustained a communal campaign to serve, shelter, and save the Jews who came knocking on their doors. "It was an unimaginable outburst of solidarity," one of the rescued told film-maker Pierre Sauvage, in his film *Weapons of the Spirit*.

Despite threats and reprisals by Nazi overlords and their Vichy collaborators, by war's end the 5,000 people of Le Chambon and its environs had saved about 5,000 Jews.[3]

"In the beginning, a few Jews made their way to this tiny corner of the world," Sauvage relates.

> And the peasants and the villagers took in the Jews who came. And the Jews kept coming. And the people of Le Chambon kept taking them in. Individuals, couples, families. The children, the elderly, people of all ages. Those who could pay and those who couldn't. Doctors and merchants and intellectuals and homemakers. From Paris and Warsaw and Vienna and Prague.[4]

Hallie writes:

> The morning after a new refugee family came to town they would find on their front door a wreath with *"Bienvenue!"* painted on a piece of cardboard attached to the wreath.[5] Nobody knew who had brought the wreath; in effect, the whole town had brought it.

> The people of Le Chambon are poor, and the Huguenot faith to which they belong is a diminishing faith in Catholic and atheist France; but their capacity to act in unison against the victimizers who surrounded them was immense. They were more than a match for their own government and for the conquerors of France.[6]

Sauvage, who grew up in New York unaware of his religious heritage until age 18, was drawn to the story of Le Chambon because it is *his* story. His parents had sought refuge in the village in the fall of 1943. "My mother was pregnant, and on March 25, 1944, a Jewish baby had the good fortune to see the light of day in a place on Earth uniquely committed to his survival."[7]

Hallie, a philosophy professor, faced Jew-bashing bullies as a seven-year-old in New Lenox, Illinois, and Hitler's armies as an artillery soldier in World War II.[8] The story of Le Chambon is, in a way, his story, too. He was drawn to the story, in particular, because it illuminates the contrasting elements of cruelty and goodness.

Why begin a book about journalism and democracy with a story of rescue from the Holocaust—a story in which journalists play no part? Beyond grappling with the Holocaust as "a foundational event of modern sensibility, forever afterward to be an essential consideration in reflections about the human condition,"[9] I am drawn to the story of Le Chambon because it brings to life many of the ideas explored in these pages. This book examines what it takes for people to rule themselves well, to make timely and wise choices in adapting to an ever-more complex and challenging universe—and then considers the role that journalism does, and might, play in creating a shareable world.

As this prologue sets out below, the history of the century past and the circumstances of the century present demonstrate that we have much to learn about self-rule, choice, and sustaining a shareable world. We need to learn quickly, given the daunting disruptions we face and our mounting doubts about whether we can escape the iron laws of history.

The story of Le Chambon is an exemplary story about people ruling themselves and prevailing against disruptions, doubts, and the brutal forces of history. It's a story of people "being in the world" by attending to what's truly important. It's a story of how a strong community can give birth to political agency, autonomy, and accountability.

To act in time

One evening during the fierce winter of 1940-1941, following the German occupation of France, Magda Trocmé, the pastor's wife, was carefully measuring the fuel she was feeding the kitchen stove in the presbytery when she was startled by a knock at the door. She opened it.

> There before her, only the front of her body protected from the cold, stood a woman shawled in pure snow. Under her shawl her clothes, though once thick, had been whipped thin by the wind and the snow of that terrible winter. But her face had been whipped even thinner by events; she was visibly frightened, and was half-ready to step back, trembling with fright and cold. The first thing that Magda Trocmé recalls seeing was the hunger in that face and in those dark eyes. Here was the first refugee from the Nazis to come to the presbytery door.[10]

When the woman asked if she could come in, Magda Trocmé reflexively responded, "Naturally, come in, and come in."

From that moment forward, André and Magda Trocmé, their family, their congregation, and their community were fully committed to saving refugees by sheltering them and by helping them get to safety in neutral Switzerland. They carried out their rescue work spontaneously, relying on improvisation and good sense. As Hallie relates, "After Magda Trocmé's first encounters with refugees, no Chambonnais ever turned away a refugee, and no Chambonnais ever denounced or betrayed a refugee."[11]

Speed was of the essence. From his experience as a soldier in the First World War, André Trocmé knew that choices "had to be made *in time*—not 'in due time,' not languorously, but in time, *now*, when the hot chain of events had not yet hardened."[12] He helped Le Chambon prepare for this time through inspiring sermons and by small steps of resistance that began soon after the Germans conquered France. The Vichy government ordered all schools to begin the day by forming a circle of students and faculty around the French flag and saluting it with the palms-down, stiff-armed, fascist salute. At the Cevenol School that Trocmé founded before the war, only those who wanted to do so made the salute, and their numbers quickly dwindled to zero. The government ordered all French school employees to sign an oath of unconditional loyalty to Marshal Philippe Petain, the head of state. No one at Trocmé's school signed. The government ordered all churches to toll their bells on the first anniversary of the Vichy regime's installation. The bell in Trocmé's church was silent.

"These refusals of blind obedience worked," Hallie writes. "Vichy did not strike, and the people of Le Chambon found themselves discovering not only that the government of France was trying to steal their consciences under the mask of loyalty, but also that they themselves could prevent the theft without being smashed in reprisal."[13]

Over time, the rescue network matured. Andre Trocmé met regularly with 13 *responsables*, young leaders of Bible study groups who also served as nodes in the network, fanning out into 13 parts of the parish. He worked with the American Friends Service Committee and the women's rescue group Cimade, which smuggled refugees to Switzerland. The Cevenol School became a haven for both refugee students and faculty. Seven group homes, primarily for young refugees, were set up during the Occupation. Boardinghouses took in refugees, as did hosts of villagers, farmers, and peasants.[14]

The continuous and expanding operations did not go unnoticed, but the Chambonnais' solidarity at times stymied the authorities. Vichy operatives considered Le Chambon a "nest of Jews." In the summer of 1942, young Chambonnais confronted Petain's visiting minister of youth about the recent roundup of 28,000 Jews in Paris, vowing never to cooperate with such an operation in their village. Two weeks later, Vichy police launched the raid that netted them only Stekler, who was eventually released as a half-Jew, and another woman whose fate is unknown. In February 1943, André Trocmé, his assistant pastor, and the principal of the public school were arrested and sent to an internment camp. They were released without explanation more than a month later, just days before the other inmates were shipped off to die in concentration camps in Poland and salt mines in Silesia. A Vichy informer came to Le Chambon and dispatched regular reports on suspicious activities until he was assassinated by the French Resistance. Shortly thereafter, in the summer of 1943, the Gestapo raided two group homes overseen by André Trocmé's cousin, Daniel Trocmé, hauling him and the young people to the death camps. That same summer, André Trocmé and his assistant, Edward Theis, went into hiding when they learned that the Gestapo had placed a price on their heads.

Still Le Chambon protected its Jewish refugees until it was liberated by French troops in September 1944. The rest of France handed over 75,000 Jews—including 10,000 children—to be deported to the death camps.[15]

Why, then, were the Chambonnais persistently willing to put "their village in grave danger of massacre, especially in the last two years of the Occupation, when the Germans were desperate"?[16]

First, the Chambonnais had a proven communal capacity for empathy and service. The village had taken in children fleeing cities during World War I and refugees from the Spanish Civil War. Rescuing the Jews was an act of religious duty that expressed not only the Chambonnais' comfort with the Jewish roots of Christianity[17] but also their regard for others:

> We fail to understand what happened in Le Chambon if we think that *for them* their actions were complex and difficult. John Stuart Mill in his essay "Utilitarianism" wrote that a benevolent person is someone who "comes, as though instinctively, to be conscious of himself as a being who *of course* pays regard to others. The good of others becomes to him a thing naturally and necessarily to be attended to, like any of the physical conditions of our existence."[18]

Second, the Chambonnais had a tradition of independent thinking. As persecuted Huguenots and as hill people, they were accustomed to following their own paths. Many of the routes from Le Chambon to Switzerland had been used by their ancestors fleeing Catholic persecution. They did not fall prey to Vichy preachments about the wisdom of collaborating with the Nazis and embracing Petain as the embodiment of the state.

Third, the Chambonnais had a workable *public*—albeit clandestine— apparatus for dealing with rescue. It was public not in the narrow sense of being derived from citizenship rights granted by the state. It was public in the broad sense of having shared objectives and shared operations in service of a larger collective—in this case, humanity in the persons of refugees. As commentator Bill Moyers observed in introducing Sauvage's film, *Weapons of the Spirit*, to broadcast audiences, this was "a whole community that made the right moral choice."[19] The public apparatus included strong leaders, communications, and continuing conversations through the church, a shared memory and identity, and, ultimately, regard for more than one's own private concerns.

Finally, the Chambonnais were *prêt à servir*—"prepared to serve"[20]— because they had worked out the fundamentals of what matters long before the Germans invaded. "We must find what we can believe, understand it, and try to act upon it when the occasion arrives," Hallie writes. "I believe that we do not have time to mystify it. On matters of ethics, we must see, understand, and choose our standards, or our lives are dark, though we may be patiently awaiting the light."[21]

In the end, the Chambonnais faced what we all face as citizens and communities—tough choices with real consequences. Pierre Sauvage ends his documentary with this testimony by Lesley Maber, who taught English at the Cevenol School for 30 years:

> Humanity is fundamentally good, with the possibility of being fundamentally bad—and this choice. It doesn't mean that bad

people are all bad and good people are all good. It doesn't mean that in Le Chambon there are not people with faults and failings. It's a community like any other community. And I think that means that any community anywhere has the choice to make and can choose right. And the people who seem very ordinary people can do great things if given the opportunity.[22]

Between past and future: the inevitable isn't

Such opportunities abound. What determines how we respond —and how effectively?

Given the challenges overcome in the century past, and the challenges pressing upon us in the century present, 40-plus years of political alienation seems a handicap we might well be rid of. What will it take to bridge the gap between people and society, between biography and history, between self and world? Can we reinfuse politics with power? Can we reclaim power through politics? Can we harness politics to help people with the struggle in their daily lives? Or is it too late? Would we just be closing the barn door after the plough horse got out?

Western thought seems torn between two notions about whether we can control our fate: free will and fatalism. We believe that free will is what shapes our individuality, gives us each a distinct identity, makes our lives particularly precious. So free will is a bedrock value. And yet, at the same time, we seem taken with notions of fatalism. The Old Fatalism centered on deities who controlled the universe, and all of us with it. The Old Fatalism foundered, mostly, with the rise of science and skepticism over religious dogma. Science and skepticism in turn gave rise to the New Fatalism. The New Fatalism holds that the laws of science are all powerful and that our actions are essentially determined by forces and patterns we have not yet fully documented—or, alternately, that skepticism fully realized demonstrates that no matter what we try to do, something will foul it up. The New Fatalism is often called *determinism*, and it is frequently qualified by a field of science (usually social science) that has laws presumed to be deterministic—economic determinism, technological determinism, historical determinism, and so on.

There is an emotional logic to both free will and fatalism/determinism. It's much more exciting and gratifying to imagine ourselves as free agents who shape our lives and our worlds as we see fit. Yet we also come to realize that our days are numbered as mortal beings—that our ends are in some sense predetermined. When we meld our sense of mortality to what science tells us about entropy in the universe— the decay of energy toward nothingness—then fatalism resonates as well.

These are more than philosophical musings. One's stance toward free will and fatalism undergirds one's sense of politics. Much of the critique of social policy regarding welfare follows a free-will line of reasoning, which argues that poor people are capable of shaping themselves into well-off people if only they had the will but that social subsidies sap them of whatever will they have. The counterargument is that poor people are trapped by forces beyond their control, leaving them with fewer resources to draw upon to rise up from poverty.

When suppositions are tacit or unquestioned, they escape scrutiny. Zygmunt Bauman writes that the neoliberal ideology that the global marketplace can resolve all questions has become the most dominant ideology in history because of "its surrender to what is seen as the implacable and irreversible logic of social reality."[23]

> Fifty years ago, in the Bretton Woods era (now ancient history), when they thought of the way global affairs were going, people in the know spoke of *universal rules* and their *universal enforcement*—of something we ought to do and will do eventually; today they speak of *globalization*—something that *happens to us* for reasons about which we may surmise, even get to know, but can hardly control. . . . "Globalization" signals a *sui generis* naturalization of the course world affairs are taking: their staying essentially out of bounds and out of

control, acquiring a quasi-elemental, unplanned, unanticipated, spontaneous and contingent character.[24]

Hannah Arendt, a thinker who will be an important presence throughout this book, holds no truck with notions of determinism. She faces up to mortality and matches it with her own bet: *natality*. Yes, we inevitably die, she acknowledges. But every time a person is born—natality—a new set of possibilities enters the world: Each person is capable of acting, and every action changes things. Given the vast numbers and varieties of people and action—the *plurality* of human existence—no one can control, or determine, the outcome of any endeavor. In consequence, Arendt rejects the notion of historical causality:

> Causality . . . is an altogether alien and falsifying category in the historical sciences. Not only does the actual meaning of every event always transcend any number of past "causes" which we may assign to it (one has only to think of the grotesque disparity between "cause" and "effect" in an event like the First World War), but this past comes into being only with the event itself. Only when something irrevocable has happened can we even try to trace its history backward. The event illuminates its own past; it can never be deduced from it.[25]

But Arendt does not succumb to the New Fatalism that our actions can have no purpose because we cannot control their ultimate outcomes. She says that we have "two islands of security" to help us manage the unpredictable nature of our actions. We can make and keep promises, which reduces uncertainty for others, and we can forgive and seek forgiveness for any unintended consequences of our actions.

> The possible redemption from the predicament of irreversibility—of being unable to undo what one has done though one did not, and could not, have known what he was doing—is the faculty of forgiving. The remedy for unpredictability, for the

chaotic uncertainty of the future, is contained in the faculty to make and keep promises.[26]

The way we, and others, respond prevents nearly anything from being inevitable—including surrendering our consciences to conquerors and collaborators. That reminder is a principal lesson Pierre Sauvage finds in the story of Le Chambon:

> I think that the world is a pretty awful place, but I think that the only way to survive the experience of living in it is to realize that *it need not be that*. And the only way to come to such a realization is to have examples. And the kids, I think, will be able in fact to absorb the magnitude of the evil if they have something to hold onto, if it doesn't sap them of their spirit. Stories like Le Chambon, stories of rescuers, are really almost like a banister which you can hold onto while looking at the evil of this world. If we don't feel deeply within ourselves that we are capable of good, we will be extremely reluctant to face the extent to which we are capable of evil, and indeed, without question, we are capable of both [emphasis added].[27]

[Manuscript ends here.]

End Notes

[1] Philip Hallie, *Lest Innocent Blood Be Shed: The Story of the Village of Le Chambon and How Goodness Happened There* (New York: HarperPerennial, 1979, 1994), 112. Hallie notes that one other person was arrested in the roundup; he could not determine whether she was deported to the death camps.

[2] Ibid.

[3] Both Sauvage and Hallie use these numbers, offered up in Sauvage's film by a refugee who forged identity papers for other refugees throughout the period. In *Lest Innocent Blood Be Shed*'s 1994 introduction, Hallie cites the village's population proper as "about 3,000" and the number of Jews saved as "about 5,000." (xiii) Elsewhere

in the 1979 text, he cites André Trocmé's notes that "about 2,500 Jewish refugees" came to the village during the occupation; Hallie adds: "I have not been able to find any way of making a sound estimate of the number." (190) Also see, Philip Hallie, *Cruelty* (Middletown, CT: Wesleyan University Press, 1969, 1982). In *Cruelty*'s 1982 postscript, he says "this village of about 3,000 people saved almost twice their number of refugees' lives."

[4] *Weapons of the Spirit*, directed by Pierre Sauvage (Los Angeles: Friends of Le Chambon Foundation,1989).

[5] Hallie, *Cruelty*, 171-172.

[6] Ibid., 170.

[7] Sauvage, *Weapons of the Spirit*.

[8] Hallie, *Lest Innocent Blood Be Shed*, 7.

[9] Jan T. Gross, *Neighbors: The Destruction of the Jewish Community in Jedwabne, Poland* (Princeton, NJ: Princeton University Press, 2001), 13.

[10] Hallie, *Lest Innocent Blood Be Shed*, 120.

[11] Ibid., 196.

[12] Ibid., 92.

[13] Ibid., 93.

[14] These details, and those that follow, come from throughout Hallie, *Lest Innocent Blood Be Shed*.

[15] Sauvage, *Weapons of the Spirit*.

[16] Hallie, *Lest Innocent Blood Be Shed*, 10.

[17] Sauvage, *Weapons of the Spirit*.

[18] Hallie, *Lest Innocent Blood Be Shed*, 284.

[19] Sauvage, *Weapons of the Spirit*.

[20] Hallie, *Cruelty*, 172.

[21] Hallie, *Lest Innocent Blood Be Shed*, 292.

[22] Sauvage, *Weapons of the Spirit*.

[23] Zygmunt Bauman, *In Search of Politics* (Palo Alto, CA: Stanford University Press, 1999), 127.

[24] Ibid., 20, 190-191.

[25] Hannah Arendt, *Essays in Understanding, 1930-1954*, ed. Jerome Kohn (New York: Harcourt Brace, 1994), 319.

[26] Hannah Arendt, *The Human Condition* (Chicago: University of Chicago Press, 1958, 1998), 237.

[27] Sauvage, *Weapons of the Spirit*, post-documentary interview with Bill Moyers.

Recalling Cole C. Campbell: A Postscript

by David Mathews

C OLE CAMPBELL'S VOICE is too unique and too important to be lost, and this collection of writings helps preserve it. The Kettering Foundation has an interest in capturing his voice because we are a research institute founded by inventors, and Cole had much in common with them. The foundation is located in one of the nation's early epicenters of innovation: it is the birthplace of powered flight and Charles Kettering's invention of the automobile self-starter. The foundation now studies civic inventors; we are always looking for the equivalents of Orville and Wilbur Wright and their flying machine. Cole was in that mold. His airplane was journalism. His landing strip was the media. And democracy, understood as a political system in which citizens govern themselves, was his navigation chart.

At Kettering, we study democracy not journalism, so I don't know much about the field; yet I sense that Cole was in a fight for the soul of his profession, a profession that is being reshaped by a multitude of forces. Cole knew that without citizens, print, audio, and visual media could be reduced to little more than vehicles for advertisement. He believed citizens were more than readers and more than consumers. What should citizens should do in a democracy? was the question that he steered by.

As his many friends and colleagues have testified, and as I wrote in the *Kettering Review* (Winter 2007), Cole was always energized and energizing, always witty, and always insightful. He had been involved in Kettering's research since the 1990s and became an associate in 2001. We were enjoying his contributions to our board, which he joined in 2006, when he died so tragically.

For our kind of research, Cole was ideal. He understood the importance of discussions that swirl around rather than proceed in a neat, straight line. These discussions are critical to developing new insights, and Cole was comfortable with the rambling give and take. He would listen carefully and then make a suggestion that reoriented everyone's thinking. After one lengthy discussion about the nature of the "public," something everyone loves to talk about but seldom defines, he proposed that the public be seen as not a thing at all, but rather as a dynamic force. It was an arresting idea. It allowed us to get beyond thinking that the public is only an audience or constituency, and we could move on to considering what a public does in a democracy. Provoking that kind of insight was Cole Campbell at his best.

Cole's concept of the public as a dynamic force continues to resonate with the foundation's work. A project at the *Virginian-Pilot*, where reporters were sent to listen to neighbors talking to neighbors, we later realized, flew in the face of the conventional wisdom that the only public is a demographically representative group. This neighborhood project assumed that no one could represent a person's truly unique, individual voice. The *Virginian-Pilot* project also recognized that people don't form their opinions in demographically representative groups. They make up their minds by talking to those they live and work with. That is the dynamic force, for better or for worse, that produces an authentic public voice.

Cole was not indifferent to the public at its worst and saw journalism as a public profession responsible for helping the citizenry make sound decisions about the future. He was one of the pioneers in taking his understanding of democracy into the newsroom. But the work he did in what was called "public journalism" was quite controversial and exacted a price. Cole understood that, yet never wavered. We are all the better for his courage. That has been especially true for the international fellows at our foundation. Journalists from Kosovo and Australia to South Africa and Colombia flocked to Cole for advice on journalistic practices that could help old and new democracies. These fellows have already written three books or monographs on the media and democracy. Although influential worldwide, Cole probably never realized just how far his influence would reach. But we do.

This volume gives us an opportunity to continue to introduce Cole to anyone who wants to make democracy work as it should.